Empires of the End-Time

Through Daniel's telescopic lens

**The uncharted end-times and
between-times of history
are laid bare in Daniel's penetrating beam.**

Charles Ozanne

ISBN: 978-1-78364-439-1

**The Open Bible Trust
Fordland Mount, Upper Basildon,
Reading, RG8 8LU, UK.**

www.obt.org.uk

Contents

****

Preface

When there are so many books and commentaries on Daniel anyone who aspires to write another should have a cast-iron reason for doing so. Surely, no better reason can be found than the conviction that one's own interpretation is more correct than other people's. That at least is my excuse for writing the present work: the belief that the exposition presented here is correct in principle, and more correct in practice, than previous efforts can lay claim to. How many other writers have made the same claim, I wonder - and been proved to be wrong! We are all so prone to error, and I am no exception. I nevertheless dare to think that the present work is on the right lines, more so possibly than other commentaries on Daniel.

A well-known critical scholar (Charles H. H. Wright) is quoted as saying, "The commentaries on Daniel are innumerable. On no other book, save the Book of Revelation in the New Testament, has so much worthless matter been written in the shape of exegesis." The same writer would doubtless dismiss my own effort as 'worthless' along with all the others he disapproves of. It all depends on one's point of view. No critical writer who takes the view that Daniel is a 'tract for the times' written in the second century BC, to encourage the faithful suffering persecution at the hands of Antiochus Epiphanes, is likely to look with favour on a work of futurist tendencies. Nor are those of futurist persuasion likely to regard with favour works of critical or amillennial tendencies.

The first thing to do, when confronted with a book of this nature, is to ask what the author believes, where he stands on various issues, to which school of thought he belongs. Is he conservative or liberal, is he amillennial or premillennial; if premillennial which point of view does he espouse? While there is much useful information to be gleaned from works liberal and amillennial, their interpretations are unavoidably very different from those of premillennial persuasion. But there are also widely differing views within the premillennial camp itself. It depends very largely on the approach one adopts.

Nearly every conservative commentator interprets Daniel in retrospect, from the viewpoint of later times. He looks at history as it subsequently occurred and finds the fulfilment of Daniel in the unfolding events of recorded history. The present work adopts an altogether different approach. It takes the view that to obtain a correct understanding of Daniel it must be seen in prospect. Its predictions should be interpreted prospectively from the viewpoint of Daniel himself, the sixth-century prophet, not retrospectively from the viewpoint of later times. Only when this is done is there any hope of grasping the prophet's meaning, but so far as I am aware no previous writer has consistently applied this approach to the book of Daniel apart from myself. My own little book *The Fourth Gentile Kingdom (in Daniel and Revelation)*, published by Henry E. Walter in 1982, does indeed anticipate the main points of the present work. But some mistaken ideas have here been corrected, and the present work goes into the whole subject in much more detail. Every chapter of Daniel has been tackled and every matter of importance has been met head on.

I have skimmed through a lot of books and commentaries in preparation for this work. Though I may not agree with most of them, I have found something of value in nearly all of them. Among critical commentaries I have found most helpful those by Montgomery and Goldingay; among amillennial (and postmillennial) those by E.J. Young and Leupold, not forgetting Keil whose knowledge of Hebrew is unsurpassed; among premillennial those by Tregelles and G.H. Lang, not forgetting Sir Robert Anderson who came close to solving the important Seventy Weeks of Daniel 9. Naturally I like best those with which I am in closest agreement, namely those in the last category.

Introduction

Babylon, Medo-Persia, Greece and what? I can just hear someone say, "What are you on about? Babylon, Medo-Persia, Greece and Rome of course." That is certainly the popular view on the meaning of Daniel 2 to be found in nearly every conservative commentary. But whence comes this unanimity that Rome is the fourth kingdom of Nebuchadnezzar's dream? It is not derived from the book of Daniel: that much is certain since Daniel never mentions Rome. It is of course derived from history. After the Greek empire of Alexander the Great the next great empire to dominate the civilised world was the Roman Empire. Hence Rome must be the fourth kingdom represented by the legs of iron. At least, so runs the argument.

It is the main contention of the present work that the methodology behind this reasoning is completely wrong. Prophecy should always be viewed prospectively, from the standpoint of the prophet himself, never retrospectively from the standpoint of history. This is the first principle of prophetic interpretation. The neglect of it always leads to error; the observance of it, if consistently applied, should lead to a correct understanding of the prophecy in question.

But it may be objected, if prophecy is a genuine foreseeing of future events, it must be fulfilled exactly as stated. And if prophecy is prewritten history, what is so wrong about finding its fulfilment in history? But I would question your premise. Prophecy is not prewritten history. It does indeed find its fulfilment in history, but not in the literal carbon-copy manner which is here implied. A.B. Davidson, in his book on *Old Testament Prophecy* (1905), contains much with which I do not agree and much else which is long-winded and boring; he did however make some wise observations on the nature of prophecy. For example he wrote as follows on the danger of regarding prophecy as a grand preview of the course of history.

> Now, we are very liable to allow ourselves in reading the prophets to be influenced by history, and to impose an interpretation on a

prophet's book which will make it a great prediction of history, or which will find, in historical events lying between the prophet and our day, a progressive fulfilment of his words. But the prophets did not write history beforehand, though, no doubt, their conceptions find fulfilment in history. Events do not always happen in the order in which they set their conceptions; at least very great spaces of time have been intercalated between occurrences which they represent as close upon one another. It is safest, therefore, to discard history, for history is as yet but a fragment; the prophet's conceptions reach out to the end of time, and here history fails us. It is also safest not to allow ourselves to be distracted by fulfilment, for the same is true of this; it is as yet imperfect, and the unequal lights which it casts upon the prophet's page disturb the eye. The conceptions of a prophet, and the way in which he connects them, may be learned from his book as from any other book; and there is nothing to hinder us from understanding him. (p.391)

In other words, the only reliable guide as to the meaning of a prophet is the prophet himself. All else, be it history or supposed fulfilment, simply disturbs the eye and leads away from what the prophet actually says and predicts. Davidson himself majored on the later chapters of Isaiah. These chapters, if read in the light of history, give rise to a scheme of prophetic fulfilment far removed from what Isaiah actually anticipated. Davidson espoused the critical notion of a Deutero-Isaiah, an otherwise unheard of prophet who is supposed to have lived during the Exile and to have authored the later chapters of Isaiah. That notion we do not accept, but that notion apart, his words are still true, in fact vital to a correct understanding of this remarkable portion of holy writ.

The horizon of Deutero-Isaiah is bounded by the restoration of Israel from exile. As events immediately following this, he describes the perfect condition of the people of God, and the evangelising of the world. This must be acknowledged to be the main conception, or vision, of the prophet. If, however, we read his words in the light of history, and suppose that his mode of representation and his disposition of events will be strictly historical, we are very apt to suppose that the order of his book will be something like this: First, a prediction of the restoration of

Israel from captivity in Babylon, such as we learn from history actually occurred; second, a prophecy of the redemption of Israel from sin through the sufferings of the righteous Servant at a time subsequent to the restoration from captivity, - a redemption which we know was effected in the death of Christ; and, lastly, some glimpses of the final glory of the people of God. This order would be that of history. But such is not the order of the prophet's book; nor is it anything like a fair description of it. For, in the first place, the restoration from Babylon, which took place historically, was in no sense such a restoration as the prophet predicted, which was a restoration of all the scattered fragments of Israel in every land. Second, the restoration he predicted does not precede, but follows the atonement of Israel's sin through the sufferings of the Servant; for this atonement is just what makes the restoration possible and is the ground of it, - the punishment of Israel, which includes the sufferings of the Servant, terminating with the termination of the Captivity.... All events are embodiments and illustrations or exhibitions of moral principles; and the restoration from captivity must be so also. That which led to the Exile was the sin of Israel - the Exile was the punishment of Israel's sin. And before Israel can be restored from captivity her sin must be forgiven. And forgiveness is based on the work of the Servant, which consequently must precede the restoration. (392 f.)

Read in the light of history, a sequence of events has been imposed on Isaiah which does indeed agree with history (as you might expect) but is nevertheless quite foreign to his own expectation of future events. For him the end of the exile in Babylon was the end of history itself as we know it and heralded the beginning of the Messianic age for which every Israelite longed. The suffering of the Servant, without which there was no forgiveness and no moral basis for Israel's restoration, must of necessity precede Israel's forgiveness and return. It must therefore, in Isaiah's conception, take place during the exile itself, not indeed in Babylon among the exiles but back at home where a Jewish remnant is still envisaged as surviving in much reduced circumstances. It is in Palestine that the Servant suffers in circumstances similar to those experienced by Christ, but at a time many centuries in advance of their actual occurrence.

Isaiah for us stands somewhere in the middle of recorded history and a very long time, about three thousand years, before the likely time of fulfilment which he describes so vividly. But for the prophet himself history was rapidly coming to a head; the consummation was not far away at all. As Davidson says, "There is really now only one step more to be taken - the Restoration: 'Israel's warfare is over, and her sin pardoned; the Lord shall lead His people home through the wilderness, and His glory shall be revealed to all flesh; and He shall feed His flock like a shepherd for ever.'"

Daniel of course was familiar with Isaiah's prophecy. Isaiah's vision of future events was also his at the beginning of his career. If the consummation seemed near to Isaiah, to Daniel it was very near, even at the doors. He had not only the inspired words of Isaiah to rest on, but those of Jeremiah and Ezekiel as well. Jeremiah he must have known as a boy in Jerusalem, and Ezekiel was a fellow exile in Babylonia. Daniel shows a particular interest in Jeremiah's prophecy that a term of seventy years had been fixed for their exile in Babylon, at the end of which period Israel would be reinstated, restored in covenant relationship with the Lord. Jeremiah's predictions simply reinforced those of Isaiah, providing specific dates for the beginning and end of Babylonian rule.

Jeremiah's prophecy of the seventy years is to be found in two places, Jeremiah 25:11-12 and 29:10. They need to be seen in the context of Jeremiah's overall forecast of future events and, more importantly, they need to be viewed prospectively from Jeremiah's standpoint, not retrospectively from the standpoint of subsequent history. The first of these prophecies was uttered in the fourth year of Jehoiakim, king of Judah, which was the first year of Nebuchadnezzar king of Babylon (Jeremiah 25:1), the year we know as 605 BC. Already, earlier in the same year, before the month of Tishri (September/ October) when Jehoiakim's third year of reign came to an end, Daniel and his companions had been deported to Babylon along with the sacred vessels from the house of the Lord (Daniel 1:1-2). In this critical year Jeremiah was given the following prophecy:

Therefore thus says the Lord of hosts: Because you have not obeyed my words, behold, I will send for all the tribes of the north, declares the Lord, and for Nebuchadnezzar the king of Babylon, my servant, and I will bring them against this land and its inhabitants, and against all these surrounding nations. I will devote them to destruction, and make them a horror, a hissing, and an everlasting desolation. Moreover, I will banish from them the voice of mirth and the voice of gladness, the voice of the bridegroom and the voice of the bride, the grinding of the millstones and the light of the lamp. This whole land shall become a ruin and a waste, and these nations shall serve the king of Babylon seventy years. Then after seventy years are completed, I will punish the king of Babylon and that nation, the land of the Chaldeans, for their iniquity, declares the Lord, making the land an everlasting waste. (Jeremiah 25:8-12 *ESV*)

The gist of the prophecy is clear. Judah and the other nations in that region were given into the hands of Nebuchadnezzar king of Babylon. The whole area would become a desolate wasteland, and all these nations would serve the king of Babylon for seventy years. But at the end of this period Babylon would itself be punished, and it too would become an everlasting waste.

The threat of desolation on Judah and the nations did not come into effect immediately. That was a threat which need not have happened at all if the nations had submitted to the yoke of Babylon (27:1-13). Zedekiah is told that he and his subjects would live if he bowed his neck under the yoke of the king of Babylon. Only if he refused to do so would his land be laid waste. This part of the prophecy did not take effect until 589 when Nebuchadnezzar ravaged the land and laid siege to Jerusalem.

Judah might have escaped the judgment of desolation by submitting to the yoke of Babylon, but there is no suggestion that Babylon itself could escape. The same expression "everlasting (or perpetual) waste" is used of Babylon in Jeremiah 51:26 ("No stone shall be taken from you for a corner and no stone for a foundation, but you shall be a perpetual waste, declares the Lord"). The fearful destruction awaiting "Babylon and the land of the Chaldeans" is rehearsed at great length in Jeremiah 50-51, and it should, according to Jeremiah 25:12, have been carried out at the close of the seventy years allocated to Babylonian rule.

Jeremiah's forecast of future events is in essence the same as Isaiah's. Isaiah predicted, and Jeremiah witnessed, the exile to Babylon, while both predicted the destruction of Babylon and the resultant restoration of Israel made possible by Babylon's fall. According to Jeremiah 29:10, "When seventy years are completed for Babylon, I will visit you, and I will fulfil to you my promise and bring you back to this place." Israel's tearful repentance and joyful return are also synchronised with the fall of Babylon "in those days and at that time" in Jeremiah 50:4 and 20. It is not simply their return to Judah, such as was authorized by Cyrus, of which Jeremiah speaks. As with Isaiah, it is Israel's final restoration prior to the establishment of the Messianic Kingdom. Their sins forgiven, their guilt removed, they are bound everlastingly to the Lord in a covenant never to be forgotten or repealed.

What therefore did Jeremiah foresee? Fulfilment in history is not our immediate concern; our concern is Jeremiah's forecast as seen through his own eyes, expressed in the words which the Lord gave him at the time. He declared first of all that Judah, along with the other nations in that region, had been given into the hands of Nebuchadnezzar king of Babylon. They were to put their necks under his yoke and to serve him obediently. Jeremiah received this message in the fourth year of Jehoiakim king of Judah, 605 BC, and it was in fact in this same year that Nebuchadnezzar overran the whole of Syro-Palestine, imposing his authority and demanding submission in the form of tribute. Judah was among those invaded. Jerusalem was besieged and captured; Jehoiakim was himself shackled with the intention of carrying him off to Babylon (2 Chronicles 36:5-7). From Daniel 1:2 it would appear that Jehoiakim actually was taken to Babylon, along with Daniel and the other Jewish captives and the sacred vessels from the Temple. Soon after however Jehoiakim was sent back to Jerusalem, having promised servile obedience to the Babylonian king (2 Kings 24:1).

This was the beginning of the judgment of Servitude. Jeremiah predicted it would last seventy years, at the end of which time Babylon and the land of the Chaldeans would themselves be punished and destroyed (Jeremiah

25:12-14). At the same time ("in those days and in that time", 50:4,20) Israel would be forgiven and restored (29:10-14; 31:30-31; 32:36-44; 33:6-26; 50:4-5,18-20,33-34). The Lord would make a new covenant with the house of Israel and the house of Judah. With the law written on their minds and hearts, they would never again disobey or go astray.

That is what Jeremiah expected to happen in accordance with the revelation granted him in 605 and subsequent years. Our next inquiry is to ask to what extent it was fulfilled. It is well documented that Babylon fell to the Medes and Persians on 12 Tishri (16 October) 539 BC, but there was no extensive damage inflicted on either the city or the land. In the words of the Cyrus Cylinder, "Without battle and conflict he (Marduk) permitted him to enter Babylon. He spared his city Babylon a calamity. Nabunaid, the king, who did not fear him, he delivered into his hand." Or, as stated in the Nabunaid Chronicle, "On the 16th (Tishri), Ugbaru the governor of Gutium and the troops of Cyrus entered Babylon without a battle."

The edict of Cyrus allowing the Jews to return to their land and rebuild their Temple was issued in Cyrus' first year according to Ezra 1:1. Cyrus' first year of reign (in Babylon) is usually given as 538, the year after his conquest of Babylon. In Daniel however this year is reckoned as the first year of Darius the Mede (5:31; 9:1). Darius may have reigned for only one year since only his first year is mentioned, in which case Cyrus' first year would be 537 as reckoned in the Bible. If it is assumed however that Darius reigned for two years, then Cyrus' first year would be 536, exactly seventy years, inclusively reckoned, from the beginning of the period of Servitude in 605.

We find therefore that the seventy years may have been precisely fulfilled so far as the return of the exiles was concerned. But even so this return was a very modest affair compared with the national (spiritual as well as physical) restoration of all the scattered Israelite fragments anticipated by Jeremiah and Isaiah. The capture of Babylon took place in 539, three years too soon, and (again) was a very tame event compared with the perennial desolation of city and land predicted by Jeremiah.

Overall, Jeremiah's predictions were not fulfilled at that time, not because he got it wrong or was uninspired, but because all prophecy is conditional on the human response, as Jeremiah himself spelt out in chapter 18:1-12. If the whole nation had repented with fasting, in sackcloth and ashes, as Daniel himself did (Daniel 9:3), the outcome might have been very different. As it turned out, Jeremiah's forecast was put on hold. A revised plan was revealed to Daniel by means of Nebuchadnezzar's dream, and even that in process of time was revised and extended, with the result that even now we still await both the destruction of Babylon (Revelation 18), and the complete restoration of Israel, national, spiritual and physical. All God's promises will be realised in the fulness of time; His gifts and calling are without repentance on His part; He is not even slow in keeping His promise as some understand slowness. He is, on the contrary, infinitely patient, not wanting anyone to perish but everyone to come to repentance (2 Peter 3:8-9).

Jeremiah's prophecy lies behind the book of Daniel. He may not have actually possessed the scroll of the law since copies were rare and accessible only to the priests. He was however in possession of some of the books (Daniel 9:2), and with the rest he was doubtless familiar. He knew Jeremiah like no other book and would have compared Jeremiah's prophecies with those he had himself received from the Lord.

William Kelly makes the same point as Davidson as to the danger of interpreting prophecy from the events of history, though he fails completely to carry it through consistently. He also makes the point, even more important, that the Holy Spirit is the only infallible interpreter of Scripture, and that only in dependence on Him is a true understanding possible.

> One of the commonest maxims, even among Christians, is this: that prophecy is to be interpreted by the event - that history is the proper exponent of prophecy - that when the prophetic visions are realized upon the earth, the facts explain the visions. This is a false principle; it has not one particle of truth in it. People confound with interpretation of prophecy the confirmation of its truth. When a prediction is fulfilled, of course its fulfilment confirms its truth, but

that is a very different thing from explaining it ...What, then, does explain prophecy? That which explains all Scripture - the Spirit of God alone. His power can unfold any part of the word of God. Do you ask, if I mean to say, that it is of no importance to know languages, understand history, and so on? I am not raising a question about learning: it has its use; but I deny that history is the interpreter of prophecy, or of any Scripture ... The understanding of Scripture is not a mere intellectual thing. If a man has no mind at all, he could not understand anything: but the mind is only the vessel - not the power. The power is the Holy Ghost, acting upon and through the vessel; but it must be the Holy Ghost Himself that fills a soul. As it is said, "They shall be all taught of God." (pp. 28-29)

Later he says, "The man who understands prophecy can open up history; but no understanding of history will enable him to explain prophecy." With that thought in mind we will embark on our exposition.

Date Chart

BC 605 Third year of Jehoiakim (Daniel 1:1).

     Nebuchadnezzar, Crown Prince of Babylon, captured Jerusalem.

     Daniel and his companions taken captive.

605/4 Fourth year of Jehoiakim.

     Jeremiah prediction of 70 years' Captivity (25:12).

603 Second year of Nebuchadnezzar (Daniel 2).

     His dream of the Great Image.

597 King Jehoiachin's Captivity (2 Kings 24:10-17).

593 The word of the Lord came to Ezekiel in Babylon (1:1-3).

589 Jerusalem under siege again (2 Kings 25:1).

586 Jerusalem fell (2 Kings 25:2-12).

     The walls broken down and theTemple burnt.

573 Ezekiel's vision of the millennial Temple (Ezekiel 40).

562 Nebuchadnezzar succeeded by Amel Marduk (Evil Merodach).

560 Amel Marduk assassinated by Nergal Sharezar (Neriglissar).

556 Nergal Sharezar succeeded by his son Labashi Marduk, but after nine months the throne was seized by Nabunaid (Nabonidus).

550 In this year probably Nabunaid went into retirement to Tema in central Arabia, leaving his son Belshazzar in charge.

     Daniel received the dream of the Four Beasts (7:1).

548 Third year of Belshazzar.

     Vision of the Ram and the He-goat (8:1).

539 Belshazzar saw the writing on the wall (Daniel 5).

     Babylon fell to the Medes and Persians (16 October).

538 First year of Darius the Mede (Daniel 9:1).

536 End of the 70 years of Servitude, 605-536 (9:2), and first year of Cyrus in Babylon.

     Cyrus decreed to rebuild the Temple (Ezra 1) but this was frustrated "all the days of Cyrus, even until the reign of Darius king of Persia" (Ezra 4:5).

534 Third year of Cyrus (Daniel 10:1).

     The last dated vision in Daniel.

520 Darius' decree to rebuild the Temple (Ezra 4:24; 6).

Work was started on the 24th day of the 6th month (Haggai 1:14-15).

In the 8th month the word of the Lord came to Zechariah (1:1).

516 The Temple was completed (Ezra 6:14-15).

458 Decree of Artaxerxes' 7th year to provide for the Temple (Ezra 7).

445 Decree of Artaxerxes' 20th year to rebuild Jerusalem (Nehemiah 2).

397 The city completed "squares and moat" after 7 year-weeks (Daniel 9:25).

331 The Perrsian Empire overthrown by Alexander the Great (8:5-8; 11:3).

In subsequent years Alexander's Empire was divided between his generals. Ptolemy secured Egypt, Cyrene, Cyprus and Palestine; Antigonus held Asia Minor; Lysimachus Thrace; Cassander Macedonia and Greece; Seleucus Babylonia.

301 Antigonus defeated at Ipsus. As a result Seleucus secured Syria and

was given Palestine.

167 The cult of Olympian Zeus was set up in the Temple by Antiochus IV (Epiphanes). This included an image of Zeus and an altar on which swine flesh was offered.

3 Jesus was born in Bethlehem.

AD 28 John began to baptise.

29 Jesus was baptised by John.

33 The Crucifixion and Resurrection of Jesus (3 and 5 April).

Structures

Daniel as a whole

A ch.1 Written in Hebrew. 3rd year of Jehoiakim. The beginning
  of Gentile domination in the experience of Daniel and his
  companions.
  B ch.2 Nebuchadnezzar's dream. Four Gentile kingdoms in historical
    succession.
    C ch.3 Daniel's companions. The fiery furnace: type of the
      Lord's people persecuted and delivered.
      D ch.4 The vision of a Tree. Nebuchadnezzar is humbled and
        restored.
      D ch.5 The appearance of a Hand. Belshazzar is condemned and
        removed.
    C ch.6 Daniel himself. The lions' den: type of Christ crucified and
      risen.
  B ch.7 Daniel's dream. Four Gentile kingdoms, future and concurrent
A chs.8-12 Written in Hebrew. 3rd years of Belshazzar and Cyrus (8:1;
  10:1). The end of Gentile domination in vision and revelation
  granted to Daniel.

Daniel 8-12

A 8:1 3rd year of Belshazzar. By the Ulai canal.
  B 8:3-14 "I raised my eyes and saw, and behold a Ram", etc.
    C 8:15-17 Gabriel speaks to him: Daniel frightened.
      D 8:18 "I fell into a deep sleep with my face to the ground".
        E 8:18-19 "He touched me and made me to stand." He said,
              "Behold I will make you to know ..."
          F 8:20-22 Persia and Greece.
            G 8:23-25 The latter end: a King of bold countenance.
            H 8:26 The evenings and mornings (2,300).
              I 8:27 Daniel went about the king's business.

              J 9:1-2 70 years to end the desolations of
                      Jerusalem.
              K 9:3-15 Daniel's confession.
              K 9:16-19 Daniel's supplication.
              J 9:20-27 70 weeks of years: on the people and
                      the holy city.

A 10:1-3 3rd year of Cyrus: by the river Tigris.
  B 10:4-6 "I raised my eyes and saw, and behold a man clothed in
          linen."
    C 10:7-8 Daniel alone saw the vision: he retained no strength.
      D 10:9 "I fell on my face in deep sleep with my face to the
              ground."
        E 10:10-11:1 "A hand touched me ... understand the words that
                      I speak to you." Also v. 18.
          F 11:2-4 Persia and Greece
            G 11:5-12:4 The kings of the North and South, and the
                      last King.
              H 12:5-12 Times and days (1290, 1335).
                I 12:13 Daniel to go his way.

Daniel One

Opportunity in Exile

The year was 605 BC, the time of year July or August. Jehoiakim, king of Judah, was now in the last quarter of his third year of reign. Nebuchadnezzar, the Crown Prince of Babylon, had just defeated the Egyptian army at Carchemish on the Euphrates and the whole of Syro-Palestine lay defenceless before him. In a few short weeks he had overrun the whole area and was now standing outside the gates of Jerusalem demanding its surrender. We are told that he besieged the city and that Jehoiakim was given into his hands (Daniel 1:2). Furthermore, Jehoiakim was bound with shackles of bronze to take him to Babylon (2 Chronicles 36:6). Whether he was actually taken to Babylon is disputed, but a literal translation of Daniel 1:2 would suggest that he was.

This verse is translated by E.J.Young, "And the Lord gave into his hand Jehoiakim king of Judah, and a part of the vessels of the house of God, and he brought them to the land of Shinar to the house of his god, and the vessels he brought to the treasure house of his god." The most obvious sense is that Jehoiakim as well as the vessels were taken to the land of Shinar (Babylonia). While both were taken to the house of Nebuchadnezzar's god, the vessels only were deposited there. Jehoiakim for his part was allowed to return to Jerusalem having promised abject obedience to the king of Babylon. According to 2 Kings 24:1 he did in fact submit for three years, but thereafter changed his mind and rebelled.

It must be significant that Babylonia is here called the land of Shinar. According to Goldingay, "In the OT, the name especially suggests a place of false religion, self-will, and self-aggrandisement (Genesis 11:1-9; Zechariah 5:11)" (p.15). Apart from Genesis and Zechariah 5:11, the name occurs only in Joshua 7:21, where Achan admits to having coveted "a garment of Shinar" and Isaiah 11:11 with reference to Israel's future exodus from their place of exile. In the present connection we think especially of Nimrod and the Tower of Babel. Daniel was not simply taken captive; he was taken captive to Shinar, the most notoriously pagan empire of the day, successor to the unspeakable Assyrians.

Daniel and his friends

Among those deported to Babylon in 605 BC were a number of young men from the royal family and nobility of Judah. They belonged to the elite of society, physically handsome and mentally alert, youths possessing the poise and self-confidence to serve (after suitable training) in the palace in responsible government posts. Prominent among these were Daniel and his three companions, Hananiah, Mishael and Azariah.

Their training was to last three academic years which in practice may not have been much more than two (cp. 2 Kings 18:9-10). If it began in the autumn of 605, it would seem to have ended by the time Nebuchadnezzar had his famous dream in the second year of his reign (603). Their studies included the language, literature and learning of Babylonia. Some of it would have been quite congenial to them, such as the grammar and cuneiform script of the Babylonian language. They would have enjoyed comparing their own language with Akkadian (the language of the Babylonians), two Semitic languages which had much in common in both syntax and vocabulary. Rather less congenial would have been the magical texts and techniques which were the stock in trade of the wise men of Babylon. The study of astrology would have been high in their curriculum. Though overlaid with superstition, there was a primitive revelation in the heavens which had been passed down from antediluvian times. This also would have been a subject of great interest to Daniel and his companions.

They were henceforth to be Babylonian in name as well as culture. Each of them was given a Babylonian name in a vain attempt to eradicate their Jewish mindset. Daniel ("God is my Judge") was called Belteshazzar, meaning "(May he) protect his life" or "May the Lady [wife of the god Bel] protect the king" (Wiseman).

As for his companions, Hananiah ("The Lord has been gracious") was called Shadrach, "Command of Aku", Aku being the moon-god. Mishael ("Who is he that is God?") was called Meshach, "Who is what is Aku?". And Azariah ("The Lord has helped") was called Abednego, "Servant of

Nebo". This was standard practice. Joseph had been given the name of Zaphenath-Paneah by the Pharaoh of Egypt (Genesis 42:45), while Esther ("Star") and Mordecai ("Marduk" or "Marduk's man") were so called by the Persian king Xerxes. In each case the name of Israel's God, El or Yah, was replaced by one signifying a Babylonian deity.

Nebuchadnezzar's aim was to mould his young protégés into the Babylonian model, both in thought and habit, but in this he was signally unsuccessful. Daniel resolved not to defile himself with the royal food and wine (1:8). This, as Lang observes, is the dominant lesson of the chapter: Daniel's resolve to shun the tempting diet which was offered to him, all the more tempting to a healthy young man in his teens. This food would have been offered to the Babylonian gods, likewise the wine, and would have included meats forbidden by the Law of Moses. So far from compromising his chances of promotion, his faithfulness in small things opened the way to his subsequent greatness. If he had not made a stand at the outset, it would have been impossible later on. Daniel's God honoured the faithfulness of His servants. He gave all four of them not only a healthier physique and complexion than all the other young men who ate at the king's table, but knowledge and understanding as well. So much so, that by the end of the course they were found to be ten times wiser than all the magicians and enchanters in the whole kingdom! And Daniel was not yet twenty!

To all four God gave learning and skill in all literature and wisdom, but in addition "Daniel had understanding in all visions and dreams" (1:17). It was not long before this accomplishment was put to the test.

William Campbell observes, "In addition to their outstanding skill, no doubt the bearing of these four Hebrew young men impressed the king; so upright, humble, transparently honest and sincere, so different from those about him, sly, cunning, wily (Daniel 2:9)" (p.9).

Daniel's long career

The seventy years of Servitude are enclosed between the first and last verses of Daniel 1, and Daniel was not finished even then. If he entered the king's service at the age of twenty, he was still there past the age of ninety (10:1). While everyone else fell victim to death or disgrace Daniel just went on and on -- through revolutions, assassinations, court intrigues, the fall and rise of empires and kings, Daniel continued. And through all these things he remained faithful to the God of his fathers, and was honoured by Him above everyone else in the whole of Babylon.

Nebuchadnezzar reigned forty-three years, 605-562 BC. His son Amel-Marduk, or Evil Merodach as he is called in the Bible, was also well disposed towards the Jewish captives. It was he who released Jehoiachin and gave him a seat of honour at the royal table (2 Kings 25:27-30). But two years later Amel-Marduk was assassinated by Nergal-Sharezar who reigned for four years. Nergal-Sharezar's son, Labashi-Marduk, had reigned only nine months when the throne was seized by Nabunaid. A few years later Nabunaid went into voluntary exile, leaving his son Belshazzar in charge of the kingdom. It was he who was killed in 539 by the invading Medo-Persians under Cyrus. Amid all this turbulence and turmoil Daniel continued.

The preposition "until" in Daniel 1:21 ("until the first year of King Cyrus") does not exclude a more remote future beyond the terminus mentioned (e.g. Psalm 110:1). Keil compares Jeremiah 1:2-3 where Jeremiah's ministry is said to have continued until the fifth month of Zedekiah's eleventh year when Jerusalem fell. But Jeremiah was still prophesying in the seventh month and for some time after that (Jeremiah 41-44). Daniel was still receiving visions in Cyrus' third year, 534 by our reckoning, seventy-one years after his capture and removal to Babylon.

Daniel Two

A Fourth Kingdom Strong as Iron

It is not my purpose to comment on every verse in the book of Daniel. There are many excellent commentaries which do just that with skill and erudition. What concerns me is the understanding of Daniel, and in this area we are badly let down by the majority of commentators. The key to understanding Daniel, as any other book of the Bible, is the consistent application of correct principles, and the most important of these is the principle of prospective interpretation. Writers such as Tregelles and Lang are among the very best and are generally correct in their understanding, but even they get it wrong through failure to appreciate the importance of viewing Daniel's visions prospectively. It is a constant temptation to read back into Daniel the known facts of recorded history on the grounds that he must have predicted what actually happened. But this temptation must be firmly resisted. Only Daniel himself, and a close attention to what is revealed, will open the way to a right understanding of this important book.

Most conservative commentators look at history first and then read back into Daniel what history records. This is the retrospective approach which invariably leads to error. The fact is, as Davidson said, "the prophets did not write history beforehand, though, no doubt, their conceptions find fulfilment in history, for history is as yet but a fragment; the prophets' conceptions reach out to the end of time, and here history fails us." This goes to show how important it is to interpret Daniel solely from the book of Daniel. A detailed knowledge of history is not required, though having decided what Daniel teaches it is certainly instructive to compare it with the facts of history. The flickering kaleidoscope of history is more often a distraction than a genuine help in our quest for prophetic truth.

Aramaic

At chapter 2 verse 4, with the words "O king, live for ever!", the Hebrew language gives way to Aramaic and remains so until the end of chapter

7. Aramaic, the language of world commerce, is appropriately used in that portion of the book which deals with Gentile powers. Tregelles says, "Now, the course, character, and crises of Gentile power are taken up in this book in the Chaldee (Aramaic) language, while those things which are limited in their application to the Jews and Jerusalem are written in Hebrew ... In the Chaldee portion we see power in the hands of the Gentiles presented before us as to its character, course, and consummation; and in the latter portion of the book we see the same power localised in connection with the Jews and Jerusalem" (Tregelles, p.7).

The Aramaic section forms a compact unit on its own. The second chapter corresponds to the seventh, the third to the sixth, and the fourth to the fifth. The emphasis is on the Gentile kingdoms which will rule the world, and the experiences of individual Gentile kings (Nebuchadnezzar and Belshazzar). Also included are the heroic stand and miraculous deliverance of Daniel and his companions when faced with death at the hands of a despotic Gentile power. A prominent theme in chapters 2-4 is the spiritual progress of Nebuchadnezzar himself from a condition of blind and arrogant idolatry to a state of mind which is best described as *conversion*.

Also written in Aramaic are parts of Ezra (4:8-6:18 and 7:12-26). Various missives to and from the kings of Persia are here recorded, and the decrees of Darius and Artaxerxes to rebuild and appoint the Temple in Jerusalem. Otherwise only Jeremiah 10:11, which contain a brief message of warning to the Gentiles with reference to their gods, is written in Aramaic.

The king has a dream

The colossal image or statue, the subject of Nebuchadnezzar's dream, is the basis of all the subsequent visions and revelations of this book. Here we can see the future course of world history as planned and prophesied at that time in all its pristine integrity and symmetry. The story is well known. The king had not forgotten his dream as implied in the older versions (*KJV* and *RV*) since the word translated "gone" in Daniel 2:5 is best understood as a Persian loan word meaning "sure". Oh no,

Nebuchadnezzar had not forgotten his dream, but he was deeply suspicious of his wise men and wanted to find out if they were genuine. Doubtless he had good reason to suspect that they were all charlatans. Their ambivalent and mechanical prognostications had failed to satisfy him. All they could offer were text book answers to text book questions (Goldingay).

Now he would find out if they had any real insight into the future. As expected, they revealed their total lack of insight (let alone foresight) by virtually admitting that they were no different from other men. "The thing that the king asks is difficult, and no one can show it to the king except the gods, whose dwelling is not with flesh" (2:11). As Goldingay well says, "The Babylonians have only earthly techniques that are no heavenly use (in the absence of data) and heavenly beings who are no earthly use" (p.54).

Nebuchadnezzar was prone to paroxysms of uncontrollable rage. On hearing this he was so furious that he ordered the execution of all the wise men of Babylon. By this time Daniel and his companions belonged to this category, and consequently search was made for them as well. It is not clear from verse 13 whether or not the slaughter had already begun. It appears to say, "and the order was published, and the wise men were slain." But the view is probably correct that the second clause is subordinate: "that the wise men should be slain."

Daniel did not panic. Though young and inexperienced he replied with wisdom and tact. He asked the king for time to consider the matter, precisely what the magicians had been denied. He asked his three companions to join him in seeking mercy from the God of heaven. We may be sure that their prayers were more than usually earnest, seeing that their lives were on the line. That very night the mystery was revealed to Daniel, a cause for praise and thanksgiving. His prayer is given in verses 20-23, the first of several in this book.

Daniel's first concern was for the lives of the wise men, not just that of himself and his friends. Arioch was doubtless relieved as well as impressed to hear Daniel's reassuring words, "Do not destroy the wise men of Babylon; bring me in before the king, and I will show the king the interpretation" (2:24). So Daniel was taken to the king. Arioch said, "I have found a man ...", as if to claim credit for himself. But Daniel claimed no credit for himself. "There is a God in heaven who reveals mysteries," he said, "and he has made known to King Nebuchadnezzar what will be in the latter days" (Daniel 2:28).

The latter days

The word "latter" ('aharith) simply means "end", and as such is the opposite of "beginning" (reshith) as in Deuteronomy 11:12, Job 8:7 and Ecclesiastes 7:8. It is used of the end of various people and things: Amalek (Numbers 24:20), Israel (Deuteronomy 32:20,29), Job (Job 42:12), the sea (Psalm 139:9), the years (Ezekiel 38:8), the indignation (Daniel 8:19), their kingdom (8:23), these things (12:8), etc.

The expression "the latter days" or better "the end of days" is an important one. It occurs fourteen times in the Old Testament and has a consistent meaning. Several commentators quote S.R. Driver's definition. It denotes, he says, "the closing period of the future so far as it falls within the range of view of the writer using it." That is a good definition so far as it goes, but as Leupold says, "to stop short at this point and to deny Messianic import to the passage is misleading.... a careful evaluation of all the passages involved shows that from the first instance of the use of the phrase (Genesis 49:1) onward the Messianic future is regularly involved." Driver himself goes on to say, "Elsewhere it is used of the ideal or Messianic age, conceived as following at the close of the existing order of things: Hosea 3:5; Isaiah 2:2 (Micah 4:1); Jeremiah 48:47; 49:39; compare 23:20 (30:24)." Here also, as the sequel shows, the establishment of the Messianic kingdom is the period principally in mind (Daniel 3:34-35, 44-45), though the closing years of the fourth kingdom (40-43) are doubtless included as well.

It is not to be inferred that the latter days had already commenced with the reign of Nebuchadnezzar, as some have done, but that the emphasis rests on the latter days. They were the days to which all the previous kingdoms were heading up, the days when the God of heaven would set up His kingdom never to be destroyed.

The dream and its interpretation

First of all Daniel reminded the king of his dream. Nebuchadnezzar must have been amazed to hear his dream narrated in every detail; he had not thought such a thing possible.

> You saw, O king, and behold, a great image. This image, mighty and of exceeding brightness, stood before you, and its appearance was frightening. The head of this image was of fine gold, its chest and arms of silver, its middle and thighs of bronze, its legs of iron, its feet partly of iron and partly of clay. As you looked, a stone was cut out by no human hand, and it struck the image on its feet of iron and clay, and broke them in pieces. Then the iron, the clay, the bronze, the silver, and the gold, all together were broken to pieces, and became like the chaff of the summer threshing floors; and the wind carried them away, so that not a trace of them could be found. But the stone that struck the image became a great mountain and filled the whole earth. (2:31-35)

And now for the interpretation:

> This was the dream. Now we will tell the king its interpretation. You, O king, the king of kings, to whom the God of heaven has given the kingdom, the power, and the might, and the glory, and into whose hand he has given, wherever they dwell, the children of man, the beasts of the field, and the birds of the heavens, making you rule over them all - you are the head of gold. Another kingdom inferior to you shall arise after you, and yet a third kingdom of bronze, which shall rule over all the earth. And there shall be a fourth kingdom, strong as iron, because iron breaks to pieces and shatters all things. And like iron that crushes, it shall break and crush all these. And as you saw the feet and toes, partly of potter's clay and partly of iron, it shall be a divided kingdom, but some of the firmness of iron shall be in it, just as you saw iron mixed with the soft clay. And as the toes of the feet were partly iron and partly clay, so the kingdom shall be partly strong and partly brittle. As you saw the iron mixed with soft clay, so they will mix with one another in marriage, but they will not hold together, just as iron

does not mix with clay. And in the days of those kings the God of heaven will set up a kingdom that shall never be destroyed, nor shall the kingdom be left to another people. It shall break in pieces all these kingdoms and bring them to an end, and it shall stand for ever, just as you saw that a stone was cut from a mountain by no human hand, and that it broke in pieces the iron, the bronze, the clay, the silver, and the gold. A great God has made known to the king what shall be after this. The dream is certain, and its interpretation sure. (2:36-45)

The only part of the statue identified here is the head of gold. "You, O king ... are the head of gold." Some have thought that Nebuchadnezzar in person is the head of gold, and correspondingly that the chest, belly and legs represent kings rather than kingdoms. But Nebuchadnezzar was head of gold only in the sense that he represented and embodied the Babylonian kingdom. It was natural for Daniel to speak in this way when addressing Nebuchadnezzar in person. But the true sense is made abundantly clear as Daniel proceeds: "After you, another kingdom shall arise."

The extent of his rule

The Babylonian kingdom was not immensely large, certainly a lot smaller than its successors. It was bounded on the east by Elam and Media, on the north by Urartu, on the west by the Mediterranean, and on the south by Egypt. Potentially however Nebuchadnezzar had been given the whole of mankind; even the beasts and birds were included in his domain. His dominion was as inclusive as that originally granted to Adam and Eve (Genesis 1:26-28) and to Noah (9:2), only the fish of the sea excepted. He could presumably have conquered the whole world if he had wanted to. In the words of Tregelles, "the only earthly bound to his empire was his ambition" (p.11). Potentially at least it was his for the asking.

Montgomery well says, "Nebuchadnezzar as the type and crown of Man has been invested with man's charter of dominion over all living creatures, Genesis 1:28, Psalm 8" (p.173). The Assyrian kings had claimed universal dominion ("King of the four quarters"), but in their case it was an empty boast. Nebuchadnezzar actually had such dominion given him by God (Jeremiah 25:26; 27:5-8; 28:14). Interestingly, he was not given dominion over the fish of the sea as Adam was. That, however, has now been given to Christ in His capacity as Son of man (Psalm 8:8), an authority He demonstrated on several occasions during His earthly ministry (Luke 5:1-11; John 21:6).

Israel had been given headship over the nations before entering the Promised Land. In Deuteronomy 28:12-13 we find, "And you shall lend to many nations, but you shall not borrow. And the Lord will make you the head and not the tail, and you shall only go up and not down, if you obey the commandments of the Lord your God, which I command you today, being careful to do them." But Israel was not careful to do them, so this headship was forfeited and transferred to a series of Gentile kingdoms beginning with Babylon. Israel however retained the spiritual leadership, though that too was forfeited later on. Neither however was forfeited for ever, since both headships, political as well as spiritual, will be restored to Israel at the second coming of Christ.

The Image in Prospect

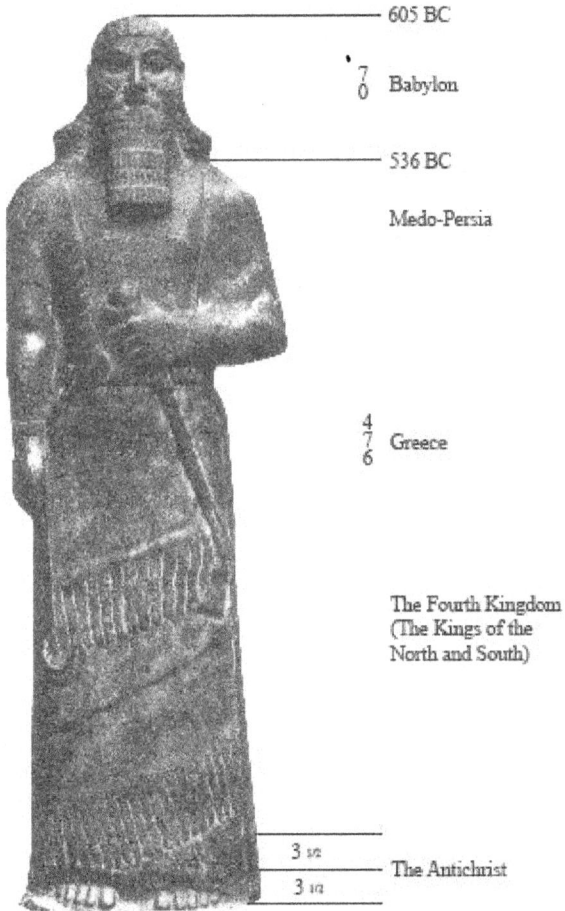

605 BC

7
0 Babylon

536 BC

Medo-Persia

4
7 Greece
6

The Fourth Kingdom
(The Kings of the
North and South)

3 1/2
3 1/2 The Antichrist

The Image in Retrospect

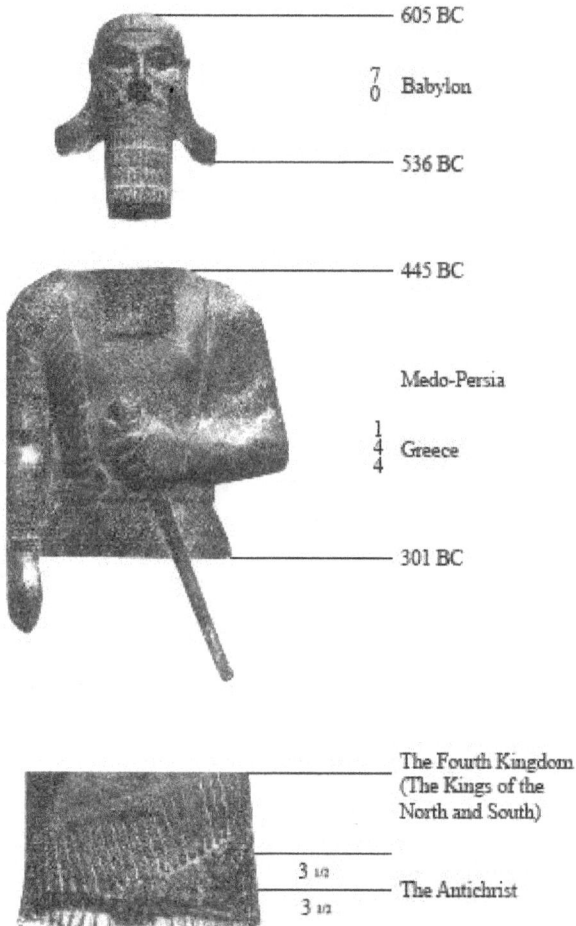

605 BC

$\frac{7}{0}$ Babylon

536 BC

445 BC

Medo-Persia

$\frac{1}{4}$ Greece
4

301 BC

The Fourth Kingdom
(The Kings of the
North and South)

3 1/2

3 1/2   The Antichrist

A single image

According to Daniel 2:31 Nebuchadnezzar saw a single image, *tselem hadh*. Very few versions even translate the word *hadh*, and many would agree with Leupold that it "apparently has no emphasis here", and is equivalent to the indefinite article. In some contexts that does seem to be the case, but not in all.

There is emphasis on this word in Daniel 2:9 ("there is but one sentence for you"); 6:2 ("three presidents of whom Daniel was one"); 7:5 ("It was raised up on one side"). The statue was one, a unified whole, as seen in prospect in Nebuchadnezzar's dream. The feet were joined to the legs, the legs to the thighs, and the body to the head. However dislocated it would eventually become in historical fulfilment, as originally seen it was one, a united image of immense proportions and terrifying appearance. But viewed in retrospect the image is far from united. The head is severed from the body and the legs are amputated at the thighs. Viewed in retrospect the image is a sad reflection of its former self. How important it is to interpret these visions in prospect before examining their fulfilment in history!

Only the first kingdom identified

The first kingdom is the only one to be identified in the second chapter of Daniel. All the others are identified in subsequent chapters but, true to the principle of prospective interpretation, it would be wrong to step beyond what is revealed at this stage.

Commentators in general do not feel any such constraint. They do not hesitate to identify all four kingdoms without further ado. Several commentators, certain that the fourth kingdom is Rome, quote Martin Luther: "In this interpretation and opinion all the world are agreed, and history and fact abundantly establish it." But as so often happens, when all the world are agreed, it is a consensus in error. The truth is of a rarer quality than to command such widespread agreement. If Daniel were writing history, albeit history beforehand, there might be justification for this opinion. But Daniel is not writing history; he is writing prophecy, and that makes all the difference. Prophecy offers an ideal view of the future, conditional to a large extent on the human response. It does indeed find fulfilment in history, but not without unpredictable delays, unexpected intercalations of time, and long postponements. History speaks with so many voices, offers so many empires to choose from; it fair mocks the student with its multiple choices. Daniel on the other hand speaks with a single voice; if we stop and listen to what he says we shall find the answer to all our questions and the identity of all the kingdoms.

A change of plan

Isaiah and Jeremiah both imply that the kingdom of Messianic fulfilment would be established at the close of the exile in Babylon. Jeremiah had even put a date to it. However, in view of what had been revealed in Nebuchadnezzar's dream, it was now clear that this programme had been radically revised. It had been superseded by another programme which seemed to stretch indefinitely into the future. Babylon would be succeeded by another kingdom, and another kingdom after that, and yet a fourth kingdom loomed on the horizon before the colossus would be finally demolished and God's indestructible kingdom established.

This change of plan had been clear to Daniel from the moment the mystery had been revealed to him. He had prayed, "Blessed be the name of God for ever and ever, to whom belong wisdom and might. *He changes times and seasons*; he removes kings and sets up kings ..." (2:20-21). The times and seasons, though fixed by the authority of the Father, are revealed to man only in part (Acts 1:7). One part was revealed to Isaiah and Jeremiah, another part to Daniel, yet another part to John on the island of Patmos. Even now we know and prophesy only in part; not till the perfect comes will the partial give way to full understanding (1 Corinthians 13:9-12).

The perfect state will not be achieved in this life, so the best we can do is to try to understand the times and seasons as currently revealed. Then like the Thessalonians, we shall not require additional instruction (1 Thessalonians 5:1).

A decrease in value but an increase in strength

Even without further instruction certain things would have been obvious to Daniel as he contemplated the vision. For one thing the metals decline in value from gold down to iron through silver and bronze. As in international sport today gold indicates the very best, then silver and bronze in decreasing excellence. But what is indicated by this downward progression? Quite a number have been suggested, but without further instruction Daniel would have noticed that the head is the only undivided part of the statue. The silver kingdom divides into two arms, the bronze kingdom into two legs, and the iron kingdom starts divided and finally splays out into ten toes.

In retrospect, a decrease in the quality of government has been noticed. Nebuchadnezzar's kingdom was an *autocracy*: "whom he would, he killed, and whom he would, he kept alive; whom he would he raised up, and whom he would, he humbled" (5:19). With the next kingdom there was less power vested in the monarch. Darius laboured till the sun went down to rescue Daniel from the lions' den, but was unable to do so because the law of the Medes and Persians could not be revoked (6:14-15). This kingdom was a *nomocracy* because the rule of law prevailed. In the case of Greece "there was an aristocracy not of birth but of supposed excellence as evinced by the power of the mind of man, and individual influence" (Tregelles). Actually Alexander's empire was a *stratocracy* since it was controlled by his generals. We have therefore a downward gradation from autocracy to nomocracy to stratocracy. This however we only know with the benefit of hindsight. Daniel himself would not have been aware of this at the time.

In the case of the fourth kingdom, there is the juxtaposition of two incompatible materials, iron and clay. Daniel's interpretation is given in 2:43: "As you saw the iron mixed with soft clay, so they shall mingle themselves with the seed of men; but they shall not cleave one to another, even as iron is not mixed with clay" (*KJV*). The verb translated "mingle themselves" is used of intermarriage in Ezra 9:2, "the holy race (seed) has mixed itself with the peoples of the lands", and this idea is certainly included in Psalm 106:34,35, "They did not destroy the peoples, as the Lord commanded them, but they mixed with the nations and learned to do as they did." To limit Daniel 2:43 to intermarriage as many do (including the *ESV*) is however too narrow. According to Keil, "The figure of mixing by seed is derived from the sowing of the field with mingled seed, and denotes all the means employed by the rulers to combine the different nationalities, among which the connubium [intermarriage] is only spoken of as the most important and successful means" (p.109).

The masculine plural determination "they shall mingle" is best explained as impersonal. They, the iron-fisted rulers, will mix themselves with the proletariat represented by the clay. They will infiltrate the masses in order to gain their support or submission. But there can be no 'marriage' between such opposites, only hostility and confrontation. Montgomery remarks, "in (the) last analysis that potter's work is but mud."

Daniel would also have noticed that the metals, while decreasing in value, increase in strength. Gold though valuable is a very soft metal, silver rather harder, bronze even harder (depending on how much zinc or tin is added to the copper), and iron the hardest of all. This would suggest an increase in brute force in the later stages, as humanitarian values give way to totalitarian. The metals not only decrease in value, they also decrease in weight or relative density. The image was certainly top-heavy, and dangerously unstable, quite apart from the admixture of clay in the feet and toes. The fourth kingdom by definition is a divided kingdom, having the firmness of iron as well as the brittleness of clay (2:42). Keil notes that the verb *palag*, divide, always in Hebrew and often in Aramaic, signifies unnatural or violent division arising from inner disharmony or discord (Genesis 10:25; Psalm 55:9; Job 38:25).

The destruction of the Colossus

When struck on the feet the image simply disintegrated. It did not even break up into shivers and shafts, but was pulverized into fragments so small that they blew away like chaff on the summer threshing-floor exposed to the wind, leaving no trace of them behind (2:35). According to Psalm 1:4, the wicked are like chaff that the wind blows away; and there are several other passages which speak in the same terms (e.g. Job 21:18; Psalm 35:5; Isaiah 29:5; Matthew 3:12). The stone responsible is seen as detached from a mountainside. The image lay directly in its path and was consequently smashed to smithereens. The stone, on the other hand, became a great mountain that filled the whole earth.

Tregelles has written, "It is almost impossible to read this chapter without remembering the words of our Lord – 'Whosoever shall fall on *this stone* shall be broken; but upon whomsoever it shall fall, it shall grind him to powder' (Matthew 21:44). The Jews fell on Christ, and they were broken (Isaiah 8); but when He returns, He falls upon the whole fabric of Gentile power, and grinds the whole to powder; then it is that His kingdom is so established as to fill the whole earth." (*The Man of Sin*, p.12.) This verse is omitted in some versions, but is included in the *ESV*, *NRSV*, and *NIV*.

But how comes it that the statue was still standing when the earlier kingdoms had all passed into history? The answer is that each successive kingdom absorbs (and adds to) the territory of its predecessors. In its final stage, the iron kingdom will include all the territory of its forerunners and a great deal more besides. Hence the rock will smash "the iron, the bronze, the clay, the silver and the gold" at a single blow. Here (v.45) the metals are mentioned in reverse order because it is the feet which are crushed first. But the clay or earthenware is place in the middle, as if to suggest that the kingdom in its final form will be brittle at the core. Though awesome in appearance and seemingly invincible, cracks will soon begin to appear. Its heart will be made of clay as well as its feet.

The statue is in human form, but only certain body-parts are mentioned. Those parts which are not mentioned, eyes, ears, mouth, hands, fingers etc., carry no significance. But those parts and limbs which are mentioned, namely arms, legs, feet and toes, must be assumed to be important in their own right. Nor do we need to be told that there were two arms, two legs, two feet and ten toes. All that goes without saying. A statue which lacked these features would not have been human in shape. These details are significant and will be explained in due course.

It says in verse 44, "And in the days of those kings the God of heaven will set up a kingdom that shall never be destroyed". But no kings have been mentioned in the previous verses. Some have thought that all the kings are meant from Nebuchadnezzar onwards, but that does not accord with the requirements of the context. The indestructible kingdom is not evolved gradually, but is set up catastrophically with the destruction of the fourth kingdom. The kings seem to refer to the ten toes which are here identified as kings. These toes are referred to as ten horns in Daniel 7:7,8 and these are said to represent ten kings in Revelation 17:12. In 2:44 we have the first intimation that this group of ten stands for ten kings.

Nebuchadnezzar's response

Nebuchadnezzar was so overwhelmed by this amazing revelation that he fell prostrate on his face before Daniel and commanded that an offering of grain and incense should be presented to him. He even paid homage to Daniel as if to a god. Paul and Barnabas had a similar experience at Lystra (Acts 14:13) and Paul in Malta (28:6). Daniel has been criticised for not protesting as Paul and Barnabas did. But Daniel was still very young and taken off his guard. He was probably too shocked and embarrassed to know what to do in face of this extraordinary exhibition so uncharacteristic of an Oriental monarch. It was in any case Daniel's God rather than Daniel himself whom the king spontaneously worshipped, as he makes immediately clear: "Truly, your God is God of gods and Lord of lords, and a revealer of mysteries" (2:47).

Prior to this Nebuchadnezzar's attitude towards the God of Israel would have been that of the Assyrian Rabshakeh in Isaiah 36:18-20. He would have regarded Him as feeble and defeated, utterly powerless compared with the victorious Babylonian gods which had conquered Judah and Jerusalem. William Campbell pictures his reaction to Daniel's oration. "We can visualise Nebuchadnezzar sitting tense; as Daniel continued his eyes widened; amazement filled his heart, the impossible was achieved; 'Yes, that was my dream exactly!'" (p.15). It is little wonder he reacted the way he did!

Daniel himself

Daniel was showered with gifts and honour. He was made ruler over the entire province of Babylon and put in charge of all the wise men. It cannot have pleased the wise men at all to have this teenage upstart from the captives of Judah placed in charge of them. Any gratitude they may have initially felt towards Daniel for saving their lives would not have lasted for long. It would very soon have been replaced by a deep-seated resentment and jealousy. Not only Daniel, but his three companions as well, were regarded with profound suspicion and intense dislike as the next chapter relates.

Daniel's meteoric rise to eminence when still in his teens is unprecedented in Bible history. Most others have had to suffer hardship for many years before being considered ready for high office. Both Joseph and David had to suffer misunderstanding and persecution before graduating at the age of thirty. Moses, having over-reacted at the age of forty, had to wait another forty years before carrying out his destiny as Israel's deliverer and law-giver. Only Daniel was ready when still in his teens, and throughout his long career he never lost that humble submissive demeanour which impresses us from the first moment we encounter him.

Conclusion

Tregelles is right when he says, "The second chapter of Daniel may be looked on as the alphabet of the prophetic statements contained in the book." Daniel 2 gives the skeleton so to speak, the rest of the book puts flesh on that skeleton. Here is the artist's initial drawing, in the rest of the book we are presented with the finished picture. So far only the head has been identified; subsequent chapters explain the rest of the image.

Daniel Three

The Faith that mocked the Fiery Furnace

Some commentators do not include this chapter (or chapter 6) in their exposition for the reason, presumably, that these historical records are not predictive and do not contribute to an understanding of Daniel's vision of future events. This however is a mistake. The miraculous deliverance of Shadrach, Meshach and Abednego from the fiery furnace and of Daniel from the lions' den make a significant contribution to Daniel's prophetic message. The fortitude of these faithful Jews under persecution has been an inspiration and example to all those in similar circumstances, Christians as well as Jews, suffering under hostile and oppressive regimes. And this will be especially true in the future when the furnace of affliction will reach proportions never before seen in the history of that persecuted race.

Light is shed on these chapters, three and six in particular, once it is realised that Daniel is a type of Christ and his three companions, types of Jewish believers. The parallels between Daniel and Christ will be considered in their proper place; here we will draw attention to the parallels between the experiences of his three companions in the fiery furnace and that of Jewish believers in the last days. This feature has often been remarked on by futurist expositors, Walvoord for example: "The deliverance of Daniel's three companions is typical of the deliverance of Israel during the period of Gentile domination. Particularly at the end of the Gentile period Israel will be in fiery affliction" (p.92).

Understandably, those of amillennial persuasion have been far less ready to recognise this. E.J. Young for example: "The remarks in the *SRB* [*Scofield Reference Bible*] that these youths are typical of the Jewish remnant, faithful in the last days in the furnace of the great tribulation, is wholly gratuitous and devoid of any Scriptural support whatsoever"(p.92). Daniel however in all his prophecies lays particular emphasis on the time of the end, the last days (e.g. 2:28; 8:17,19; 10:14; 12:4,9). It is natural therefore to find an illustration of these days in the suffering of Daniel and his friends.

Shadrach, Meshach and Abednego had to face a literal furnace of red-hot fire. A furnace, less literal though no less real, has been the experience of the Jewish people on many occasions. Their affliction in Egypt is compared to an iron-smelting furnace in Deuteronomy 4:20; 1 Kings 8:51, and Jeremiah 11:4. Their suffering in Babylon, both present and future, is called "the furnace of affliction" in Isaiah 48:10. And their future deliverance is likened to walking through the fire, in which however "you shall not be burned, and the flame shall not consume you" (Isaiah 43:2). Anyone having to face this ordeal will find encouragement and instruction in the steadfast example of Shadrach, Meshach and Abednego.

The golden image

Nebuchadnezzar made an image of gold ninety feet high and nine feet wide. This immense statue he set up in the plain of Dura not far from Babylon. It must have been clearly visible for miles around, its imposing frame glinting in the sunlight for all to admire and worship. It was designed to be the focal point of the Babylonian empire itself, a magnet to attract and unite all the nations in reverential awe of Babylon the great and its majestic builder. Like the Tower of Babel in the plain of Shinar it seemed to reach to the heavens and was calculated to make a name for Nebuchadnezzar this latter-day Nimrod.

The statue was probably made of wood overlaid with gold plates on the same principle as the altar of incense (Exodus 37:25-26). This method was used in the manufacture of idols as described in Isaiah 40:19; 41:7 and Jeremiah 10:3-4. A man's height is only four or five times his average width, but this statue was ten times its width. This prompts William Campbell to ask, "Was it a human form elevated on an elaborately terraced pedestal? or was it a Serpent?" Several writers have observed that at Tolul Dura ('Mounds of Dura'), twelve miles southeast of Hillah, a large brick plinth has been found, 20 feet high on a 45 feet square base . This was found by archaeologist Jules Oppert and could be the base of Nebuchadnezzar's image. The river Dura flows into the Euphrates some six miles south of Babylon.

Its significance

Commentators are not agreed as to what this statue was supposed to represent. According to Keil, it was "the symbol of world power established by Nebuchadnezzar." According to Lang, "The Babylonian empire, the golden image, was the expansion of its Founder, the head of gold, and he was the embodiment of it. To honour it was to honour him, and by requiring all men to worship the image, the State, he secured that they should worship himself, its creator, genius and inspiration." Goldingay remarks, "Whatever the nature of the statue, it held religion and state together. The institution that claims absolute authority is inclined also to claim the sanctions of religion." D.J. Wiseman observes, "If the image was not of the king claiming obeisance as 'king of kings' (Daniel 2:37-38) then it would be expected to represent the city-god Marduk" (p.109). That the statue was of the deified Nebuchadnezzar was first advanced by Hippolytus, the first Christian commentator on Daniel, c. 200 AD.

There is doubtless a connection between this towering statue of gold and the dream-image of Daniel 2 of which Nebuchadnezzar was the head of gold. Evidently the king had been pondering his own exalted role as head of gold. In his ego-inflated imagination he had ceased to be just the head and had become the entire image all made of gold. Although no date is recorded, the occasion was probably not long after his dream. The statue stood for himself as the embodiment of the Babylonian empire and the representative of the gods of Babylonia. To bow down to the statue would be tantamount to worshipping the gods which it and he represented, just as Nebuchadnezzar had himself acknowledged Daniel's God when he fell prostrate before him (2:46-47).

The penalty for not worshipping the image

The penalty for refusing to worship the image was to be incinerated in the burning fiery furnace. Leon Wood pictures the furnace placed ominously near the image in full view of the assembled officials, with flames leaping menacingly out of the top opening. But this is probably fanciful. Nebuchadnezzar was not looking for or expecting martyrs. He was not asking anyone to abandon his own gods or mode of worship, only to bow down to his golden image in recognition of Babylon's imperial might and the proven superiority of the Babylonian gods. There was no reason why anyone should refuse, except of course the Jewish captives who had an express command from God not to bow down or worship any idol in any conceivable shape or form (Exodus 20:4-6).

Wiseman throws light on the nature of the kiln. "Massive furnaces", he says, "must have been used to fire the estimated fifteen million kiln-fired, as well as glazed, bricks required for Nebuchadnezzar's numerous building operations. These were usually fired to about 850-950 centigrade but a higher temperature could be obtained by the use of wood fires or the equally available bitumen from Hit" (p.112).

The Babylonians were experts in the art of brick making and the chemistry of ceramic glazes, as shown for example in the age-enduring luminous blue Ishtar Gate. Ron Cantrell says, "If one can make a glaze that would withstand the harsh desert elements for millennia, they must have been adept at the craft. A kiln hot enough to bake bricks and melt silica and the chemistry used to make glazes is a furnace hot enough to make glass" (p.82).

Who were invited?

According to R.A. Anderson, "The invitation list for such an occasion was necessarily a lengthy one including, for reasons of protocol if for no other, every conceivable category of officialdom from ministers of state to provincial chiefs" (p.30). There were other Jewish captives in Babylonia besides Shadrach, Meshach and Abednego, but they were not government officials, and were not therefore faced with the same dilemma. The question remains, however, why there is no mention of Daniel. Some have suggested that he might have been sick or absent on official business, but there are other possibilities which are far more likely.

In the view of R.H. Charles, Daniel was excused by reason of his seniority, his elevated position. "Whereas at the close of ch.2 the three companions are rewarded with high official appointments, Daniel is clearly set above all the wise men and governors of Babylon; for he sits in the king's gate (2:49), i.e. as the Vizier or Prime Minister of the king, and so is not exposed to the risks that his three companions encounter in ch.3" (p.23).

I doubt however if that would have excused him. It is more probable, in my view, that the Chaldean astrologers who denounced Shadrach, Meshach and Abednego prudently refrained from exposing Daniel though he too had been guilty of the same offence. Daniel had the ear and favour of the king who still held him in high esteem. To have reported him would almost certainly have backfired on his accusers and led to their own disgrace. Careful not to overreach themselves, they wisely levelled their calumnies at Daniel's more vulnerable friends who occupied less exalted positions. Daniel had his own ordeal to face later on: in this chapter the spotlight falls on his heroic friends.

The king's fury

Nebuchadnezzar did not immediately impose the prescribed punishment on the three disobedient young men. He gave them another chance to comply just in case they had been wrongly accused by their jealous detractors. When however they answered defiantly and still refused to obey, the king flew into a rage. It has been said that Nebuchadnezzar's rage got the better of his reason when he ordered the furnace to be heated seven times more than usual. Would it not have made more sense to *reduce* the heat seven times if his purpose was to inflict a more agonizing death on his unrepentant victims? But was that in fact his purpose at all?

If we read his mind correctly, Nebuchadnezzar's argument was not so much with Shadrach, Meshach and Abednego as with their God. "If the God of the Jews was going to intervene, Nebuchadnezzar was determined to thwart him at every turn" (R.A. Anderson). It was intervention by their God which the king feared most of all and which he planned to forestall. There would be little chance of divine intervention, he thought, if his victims were to die before their God had time to react.

So he did his best to ensure their instantaneous death before even reaching the furnace if that were possible. He was of course greatly mistaken if he thought he could catch God off His guard, but

Nebuchadnezzar at this stage had a very meagre understanding of the power and wakefulness of the God he was dealing with!

The outcome

The resolute faith of the three young men was richly rewarded. As Leupold says, "These men ask for no miracle; they expect none. Theirs is the faith that says: 'Though He slay me, yet will I trust Him', Job 13:15." These three "quenched the power of fire", but there were others of equal faith who were stoned, sawn in two, and killed with the sword (Hebrews 11:34-38).

There were a number of things that amazed the king. These men were free; they were walking about in the fire; not even their clothes were on fire, let alone themselves; and there were now four of them not three, and the fourth was like a son of the gods! The Lord had sent His angel to protect them as promised in Psalm 91:9-12.

There were also far-reaching results. Not only were they miraculously delivered, completely unscathed and even unscorched from the fire which killed instantaneously the strong men who put them there, but their God is acknowledged and extolled by the incredulous king himself. He now calls them "servants of the Most High God" and blesses "the God of Shadrach, Meshach and Abednego, who has sent his angel and delivered his servants, who trusted in him, and set aside the king's command, and yielded up their bodies rather than serve and worship any god except their own God."

Nebuchadnezzar is not yet a converted man. It is nevertheless the God of Israel who is worshipped and adored, not the tawdry gold statue which has now lost its lustre, shown up for the sham that it is, a toothless giant with feet of clay. Furthermore, Nebuchadnezzar issued a decree that "Any people, nation, or language that speaks anything against the God of Shadrach, Meshach and Abednego shall be torn limb from limb, and their houses laid in ruins, for there is no other god who is able to rescue in this way."

The religion of the Jewish captives has now official recognition. They can worship in the way they were accustomed without fear of reprisal or punishment. Moreover this decree was promulgated throughout the empire. Leon Wood asks, "People everywhere, including the Babylonian priests, would read the decree, and what would they think?" They can hardly have been pleased! Their scheme to bring down Shadrach, Meshach and Abednego had badly backfired! The Jewish faith was now a *religio licita*, a permitted religion, as it was under the Persians and later under the Romans.

A.E. Knoch says, "Not only does the government demand respect for the God of the Jews, but, in the province of Babylon, they are placed under a special government bureau, composed of the triumphant trio who had passed through the flames for their faithfulness. Satan overreached himself. He turned the government in their favour, rather than against them" (p.103).

What of the future?

Religious freedom, freedom to worship God as one wishes, is quite a recent idea. It did not exist in any ancient civilization and does not exist in most countries today. Our protestant forefathers, having won their own freedom from the Catholic state-religion, straightway denied this freedom to those who disagreed with them. "Religion and the State get intertwined. Refusal to worship the image cannot be tolerated because it subverts the authority of the State" (Ernest Lucas).

Even dictators, who have renounced the religion of their forefathers and admit to no belief in God at all, have in practice turned the State into God and themselves into the embodiment of the State. Images of themselves are placarded in every public place, and statues of themselves in every city square. Dissenters who do not bow down to this god are routinely persecuted and martyred for their faith. As A.E. Knoch says, "whenever the state controlled religion, or religious dignitaries [controlled] the state, the result has usually been a fiery furnace for those who dissent."

The iron kingdom of Daniel 2 will be a totalitarian state of the most intolerant kind. It does not seem that any traditional religion will be recognised, not at least by the Antichrist himself. His brazen effrontery in matters of religion is outlined in Daniel 11:36-39. He will exalt and magnify himself above every god and speak astonishing things against the true God. He will pay no attention to the god of his fathers, but will magnify himself above all. Specifically, he will honour the god of fortresses, and will honour this god with gold and silver and precious gifts. Hence his god will be a reflection of himself, a god of military might and oppression.

His adjutant, the beast out of the earth, will deceive those who dwell on the earth, "telling them to make an image for the beast that was wounded by the sword and yet lived." He is even enabled to give breath to the image of the beast, causing it to speak and to kill all those who refuse to worship the image. Only those who agree to be marked (or tagged) on their right hand or forehead will be permitted to buy and sell (Revelation 13:14-17).

This is the tendency of all totalitarian regimes and the antichristian regime of the future will be the ultimate in totalitarian regimentation. It is moreover this very situation which is anticipated in Daniel 3. Nebuchadnezzar's image of gold is the forerunner of the image of the beast, Shadrach, Meshach and Abednego the prototypes of all those who refuse to bow down before the State religion and its fabricated god.

Daniel Four

Chop down the Tree

Here in Daniel 4 we have one of the most remarkable documents of ancient times, a proclamation unique among the archives of Oriental kings. According to Montgomery, "As an edict the document is historically absurd; it has no similar in the history of royal conversions nor in ancient imperial edicts." But for us it provides a powerful testimony to the grace and mercy of our God in the conversion of a proud and disobedient king.

Verses 1-18 and 34-37 are in the first person, the reported speech of Nebuchadnezzar himself. He fearlessly publishes his experiences to "all peoples, nations, and languages, that dwell in all the earth." He offers praise to God; he describes the alarming dream he had received; he tells how his reason returned to him at the end of the days; he again blesses the Most High, and explains how even more greatness was added to Him, giving the credit and honour due to the King of heaven. This amazing testimony to the grace and power of the Most High God was circulated throughout his vast domains.

The intermediate verses, 19-33, describe in narrative form Daniel's interpretation of the dream and the manner of its fulfilment. This forms no part of Nebuchadnezzar's confession, but is necessary for the understanding of what happened.

The dream itself

The king states at the outset his intention "to show the signs and wonders that the Most High God has done for me." The signs were the amazing dreams he had received, both here and in Daniel 2; the wonders include the fulfilment of the current dream in his madness and remarkable recovery at the precise time indicated by the dream.

He then records the circumstances under which he received the dream. He was, he says, at ease in his palace, prospering like a hot-house plant in the full ebullience of its foliage. Many years, it seems, had passed since the events described in chapter three. He had now reached the apex of his achievement. His kingdom was at peace, his building operations near completion. "It seems", says A.E. Knoch, "that Nebuchadnezzar had fallen into a self-complacent, self-satisfied, somnolent condition, inflated by his own greatness, utterly oblivious to God's supremacy." His earlier dream and even the miraculous deliverance of Shadrach, Meshach and Abednego were distant memories that no longer exercised his conscious mind. They had indeed made a deep impression on him at the time, but he now wished to distance himself from Daniel's God, who made impossible demands on him which he, as king of Babylon, could not possibly fulfil.

It was in these circumstances that God once again intervened in his life. His first dream had deeply troubled him, depriving him of sleep (2:1); this one had an even more dramatic effect on him. It not only made him afraid, but worked on his emotions with forebodings of future nemesis which profoundly disturbed him. He summoned the wise men of Babylon without delay. This time he made no attempt to hide what he had seen.

> The visions of my head as I lay in bed were these: I saw, and behold, a tree in the midst of the earth, and its height was great. The tree grew and became strong, and its top reached to heaven, and it was visible to the end of the whole earth. Its leaves were beautiful and its fruit abundant, and it was food for all. The beasts of the field found shade under it, and the birds of the heavens lived in its branches, and all flesh was fed from it. I saw in the visions of my head as I lay in bed, and behold, a watcher, a holy one, came down from heaven. He proclaimed aloud and said thus: "Chop down the tree and lop off its branches, strip off its leaves and scatter its fruit. Let the beasts flee from under it and the birds from its branches. But leave the stump of its roots in the earth, bound with a band of iron and bronze, amid the tender grass of the field. Let him be wet with the dew of heaven. Let his portion be with the beasts in the grass of the earth. Let his mind be changed from a man's, and let a beast's mind be given to him; and let seven periods

of time pass over him. The sentence is by the decree of the watchers, the decision by the word of the holy ones, to the end that the living may know that the Most High rules the kingdom of men and gives it to whom he will and sets over it the lowliest of men. This dream I, King Nebuchadnezzar, saw. (4:10-18)

The dilemma of the wise men

The meaning of the dream is really rather obvious. As Goldingay remarks, its interpretation requires little more than Nathan's "You are the man!" (2 Samuel 12:7). This makes the wise men's avowal that they were unable to interpret it somewhat perplexing. But we need to understand the dilemma in which they found themselves. "Should they seek to flatter the grand monarch by making him the great tree, they must, at the same time, give grave offence by predicting his degradation" (Knoch). This is something they dared not do, for fear the grand monarch might fulminate with rage and order their execution as he had done once before. They chose therefore the course of discretion and professed not to know what the dream signified.

Daniel's late arrival on the scene has been explained in various ways. The Septuagint avoids the problem by leaving out verses 6-10a. This, says Charles, "puts the action of the king in a reasonable light." But a text which simply omits the offending verses is obviously secondary. Others have agreed with Calvin that Nebuchadnezzar as yet wanted no dealings with Daniel's God, and so consulted first all the other wise men. There is however nothing in the text to suggest that Daniel was bypassed or overlooked. More probably it was Daniel's own decision to allow the wise men to have the first opportunity to interpret the dream. He was not one to push himself forward, though as "chief of the magicians" he had the right to do so. We may be sure that the college of wise men deeply resented Daniel's promotion over their heads. He was therefore careful at all times to treat them with deference and respect in order to avoid offending them. It was in any case better to be asked by the king to interpret the dream after the wise men had failed, than to risk their displeasure by speaking up first.

Nebuchadnezzar and all the trees

The magnificent tree situated in the midst of the earth is of course Nebuchadnezzar himself. The tree literally dominated the world. Its top reached the heavens (like the Tower of Babel, Genesis 11:4), and it could be seen the world over. It provided food and protection for creatures of every kind. The command is then given to cut it down, lop off its branches, and strip off its leaves.

The picture is a familiar one. In Ezekiel 31 Assyria is compared to just such a tree, a luxuriant cedar in Lebanon. That tree also had its top among the clouds, the birds made their nests in its boughs, and under its branches the animals nurtured their young. But because it towered so high, set its top among the clouds and was proud of its height, foreigners had cut it down and left it. The once magnificent cedar now lay strewn across the mountains and valleys, broken and abandoned. This moreover was the fate awaiting Pharaoh King of Egypt and every other tree which boasted of its glory and greatness.

Of all the nations compared to trees one thinks especially of Israel. John the Baptist had warned them, "Even now the axe is laid to the root of the trees. Every tree therefore that does not bear good fruit is cut down and thrown into the fire" (Luke 3:9). Our Lord took up the same theme in Luke 13. A man had a fig-tree planted in his vineyard, and he came seeking fruit on it and found none. The command is then given, "Cut it down. Why should it use up the ground?" This tree (like Nebuchadnezzar, Daniel 4:20-22), was given one more year in which to bear fruit before being cut down (13:6-9).

So Nebuchadnezzar, like Assyria and Israel, was to be cut down by reason of his pride. But his downfall would not be total or permanent, for the stump and roots of the tree were to be left in the earth, bound with a band of iron and bronze, amid the tender grass of the field, and in this condition "seven times" would pass over it (4:15-16).

This also is a familiar theme in the Bible - the idea of a stump being left which would subsequently spring back to life and resume its former glory. Isaiah is warned that his preaching would fall on heavy ears and blind eyes. Israel would inevitably be destroyed and forsaken. Though only a tenth remain in it, it will be burned again. Nevertheless, it will be "like a terebinth or an oak, whose stump remains when it is felled. The holy seed is its stump" (Isaiah 6:13).

In the same way, "There shall come forth a shoot from the stump of Jesse, and a branch from his roots shall bear fruit" (Isaiah 11:1). Jesus, through His only human parent, was descended from Nathan, a junior branch of the house of David which bypassed all David's royal successors including Solomon (Luke 3:31; 2 Samuel 5:14; Zechariah 12:12) - a true shoot from the stump of Jesse. As Job said:

> For there is hope for a tree, if it be cut down, that it will sprout again, and that its shoots will not cease. Though its root grow old in the earth, and its stump die in the soil, yet at the scent of water it will bud and put out branches like a young plant. (Job 14:7-9)

The band of iron and bronze

There was no question of Nebuchadnezzar's stump dying in the soil since it was to be "bound with a band of iron and bronze." Commentators are not agreed over the meaning of this imagery. Young gives five possible interpretations, four of them fanciful and one only partially correct. Ernest Lucas speaks for many in saying, "the most plausible interpretation of the 'band of iron and bronze' is that it is part of the shift of imagery, and refers to the demented king being restrained in fetters." But Nebuchadnezzar did not act like a wild animal which needed to be restrained with fetters. He behaved like a harmless ruminant browsing in the palace meadow.

The band either encircled the stump to prevent it from splitting, or formed a low fence to keep away animals and undergrowth. It might even have encased the whole stump to prevent it from rotting. In any case its purpose was to protect the stump from damage or decay. The plain sense is that Nebuchadnezzar's kingdom would be protected and preserved pending the king's return to sanity (see 4:26). Invariably in the Bible iron and bronze signify durability, impervious hardness, stubborn obstinacy, irresistible power and the like. The references speak for themselves.

Leviticus 26:19 "I will make your heavens like iron and your earth like bronze" (likewise Deuteronomy 28:23).

Deuteronomy 33:25 "Your bars shall be iron and bronze" (Moses' blessing to Asher).

Job 40:18 "His bones are tubes of bronze, his limbs like bars of iron" (Behemoth).

Job 41:27 "He counts iron as straw, and bronze as rotten wood" (Leviathan).

Psalm 107:16 "He (the Lord) shatters the doors of bronze and cuts in two the bars of iron" (likewise Isaiah 45:2).

Isaiah 48:4 "your neck is an iron sinew and your forehead brass" (of Israel's obstinacy).

Jeremiah 1:18 "Behold, I make you this day a fortified city, an iron pillar, and bronze walls, against the whole land ..." (Jeremiah himself).

Jeremiah 6:28 "They are all stubbornly rebellious ... they are bronze and iron, all of them act corruptly."

Jeremiah 15:12 "Can one break iron, iron from the north and bronze?"

Micah 4:13 "Arise and thresh, O daughter of Zion, for I will make your horn iron, and I will make your hoofs bronze..."

Daniel 7:19 "its teeth of iron and claws of bronze" (the fourth beast).

Thus was the kingdom preserved for Nebuchadnezzar and Nebuchadnezzar for the kingdom. His throne was as secure as only iron and bronze could make it.

The seven times

This brings us to the seven times which would pass over Nebuchadnezzar (4:16,23). Only in Leviticus 26 (vs.18,21,24,28) do the words "seven times" occur in the *KJV*, but this translates the single word "seven" and the meaning is "sevenfold". Far closer to Daniel's seven times is the "time, times, and half a time" of Daniel 7:25 and 12:7. The same expression appears in Revelation 12:14 where it is evidently the same period of time as the 1260 days of 12:6. In Daniel, "time, times and half a time" is the period granted the little horn to wear out the saints of the Most High (7:25), and for shattering the power of the holy people (12:7). If this corresponds to the second half of the Seventieth Week, Daniel 9:27, as seems to be the case, we have a sound reason to agree with the

Septuagint that the seven times are equivalent to seven years.   This, I believe, is the true significance of the seven times, and Daniel also must have arrived at the same conclusion without the benefit of subsequent revelation. Without that understanding he would not have known when to expect Nebuchadnezzar's recovery. But with it he could have advised the rulers of Babylon of the exact time to the very day. One can imagine what lavish preparations would have been made to welcome him back to his palace and throne! A public holiday, a magnificent reception, an extended period of celebration and rejoicing! Preparations would have begun months in advance because the day had been known long beforehand. In the meantime an interim government, a regency maybe, would have been set up, but there was no move to replace the king with another since they knew exactly how long his illness would last.

Daniel's counsel

Daniel concluded his recital by daring to counsel the king. "Therefore, O king, let my counsel be acceptable to you: break off your sins by practising righteousness, and your iniquities by showing mercy to the oppressed, that there may perhaps be a lengthening of your prosperity" (4:27). This required enormous courage on the part of Daniel, and it may not have been well received. As Farrar remarks, "the absence of any mention of rewards or honours paid to Daniel is perhaps a sign that he was rather offended than impressed."

Nebuchadnezzar had applied himself and his resources toward building a magnificent city as a monument to himself and his empire, but alleviating the poor was not included in the programme. Doubtless many hundreds of captives had suffered and died carrying out his grandiose plans. It was only the end result which he cared about, not the living and working conditions of his slave labour force. This was something he preferred not to be reminded about. To God however it was a matter of deep concern, second only to Nebuchadnezzar's insatiable pride.

The outcome

The prophecy was fulfilled twelve months later. Nebuchadnezzar was on the roof of his palace admiring the fabulous city which he had built. As he gazed around at the temples and palaces, the incredible hanging gardens, the walls and ramparts, the lakes and fountains, his heart was lifted up in self-exalting pride. In this inflated frame of mind he uttered the fateful words, "Is not this great Babylon, which I have built by my mighty power as a royal residence and for the glory of my majesty?" (4:30).

At that very moment, while the words were still in his mouth, the judgment came into effect. His countenance changed, his reason departed, he growled and grunted like an animal. His frightened courtiers hustled him out of the palace, where in the garden he began to chew grass like an ox. And there he remained for seven long years, until he had learned the hardest lesson of all, "that the Most High rules the kingdom of men and gives it to whom he will." As Campbell observes, "The first dream which God imposed on Nebuchadnezzar led him to world headship; the second dream reduced him to the level of a beast."

The disease he suffered from is known as Lycanthropy, or in his case Boanthropy, the mental disorder which causes a man to think and act like an ox. Pusey remarks, "not even the extreme form of insanity interferes with the inner consciousness, or, consequently, with the power of prayer." "The inner consciousness remains unchanged, while, up to a certain point, the sufferer thinks, speaks, acts, as if he were another." In his more lucid moments Nebuchadnezzar would have understood what had happened to him, why it had happened, and what was required of him to repair the situation and relieve his condition.

Walvoord cites an actual case very similar to Nebuchadnezzar, which he found in Raymond Harrison's *Introduction to the Old Testament*, pp. 1116-17. Part of the description is as follows:

> His mental symptoms included pronounced anti-social tendencies, and because of this he spent the entire day from dawn to dusk outdoors, in the grounds of the institution.... His daily routine consisted of wandering around the magnificent lawns with which the otherwise dingy hospital was graced, and it was his custom to pluck up and eat handfuls of the grass as he went along. On observation he was seen to discriminate carefully between grass

and weeds, and on inquiry from the attendant the writer was told the diet of this patient consisted exclusively of grass from hospital lawns. He never ate institutional food with the other inmates, and his only drink was water ... The writer was able to examine him cursorily, and the only physical abnormality noted consisted of a lengthening of the hair and a coarse, thickening condition of the finger-nails. Without institutional care, the patient would have manifested precisely the same physical conditions as those mentioned in Daniel 4:33.

His restoration and conversion

In Daniel 2-4 we have the record of God's working in Nebuchadnezzar's life, resulting in his conversion from polytheistic idolatry to worship the one true God. Those who deny that he was a truly converted man have not appreciated the unique significance of Daniel 4 nor the power of God to save the most notorious of sinners. Here we have the monarch of the greatest empire the world had ever seen proclaiming to "all peoples, nations and languages, that dwell in all the earth" the fact that he now "blessed the Most High, and praised and honoured him who lives for ever, for his dominion is an everlasting dominion, and his kingdom endures from generation to generation..." (4:34).

Goldingay poignantly comments, "Nebuchadnezzar, lord of a worldwide empire, sends word round his empire, and his subjects wonder what further demand or obligation is to be placed on them. The contents of his message confounds their expectations. The communication ceases to be an encyclical and becomes a testimony such as we read in the Psalms, of a man whom God has marvellously rescued from some calamity, who now makes public confession of the wonders God has performed for him and offers the praise that recognizes how his power extends beyond this one moment to the whole of history" (pp. 90-91).

In chapter 2 Nebuchadnezzar acknowledged that Daniel's God is "God of gods and Lord of lords, and a revealer of mysteries", that is a god more powerful than any other in his pantheon. In chapter 3 he forbade anyone to speak against the God of Shadrach, Meshach and Abednego on pain of draconian punishment - "for there is no other god who is able to rescue in this way." In chapter 4 there is no limit to his praise of the Most High God. His dominion is both worldwide and age-abiding; His will absolute among the host of heaven as much as the inhabitants of the earth; His actions without let or hindrance, non-accountable to anyone. "How striking", exclaims G.H. Lang, "are the last words of Nebuchadnezzar, as far as Scripture records them: 'Now I Nebuchadnezzar praise and extol and honour the King of heaven: for all His works are truth, and His ways judgment: and those who walk in pride He is able to abase'" (p.37).

It is true he does not specifically mention his sins and need for repentance, but that would hardly have been appropriate in a document of this nature. It is God's greatness he wished to declare, not his own wretchedness. He does however mention the need for humility (vs.17,37), this being the particular area in which he himself had failed.

Daniel Five

A Godless Feast and the Finger of God

It is no accident that this chapter, Daniel 5, follows the previous one. Though they are probably separated by some considerable time, in point of subject matter they are very similar. In the one case a proud and presumptuous king is humbled to the extent that his mind and behaviour are those of a domesticated ox; but having learned his lesson he is restored to his former glory, in fact his greatness even exceeded the greatness he had previously known. In the other case, an equally proud and presumptuous king, who adds profanity and sacrilege to his other failings and shows no disposition to repent, is summarily cut off.

These two chapters are the central pair in the Aramaic portion of Daniel, and indeed central to the structure of the book as a whole. To the writer of Daniel they constitute the most important part of his message: the profoundly sinful nature of pride coupled with profanity, and the likely retribution for such pride whether remedial or punitive. Daniel 4 ended with the words "those who walk in pride He is able to humble." Nebuchadnezzar speaks from bitter experience. It had taken an extreme measure to cure him of his pride, but now he honours and extols the God of heaven, and is unashamed to declare to the whole world that "all his works are right and his ways are just; and those who walk in pride he is able to humble."

The sacred vessels

All this Belshazzar knew (5:22), but Belshazzar had completely failed to take it on board or apply it to himself. On the contrary, he had turned his back on Daniel's God - and Daniel as well, it would seem. He praised instead the gods of gold and silver, bronze, iron, wood and stone. These dumb idols were for him more powerful than the God of Israel, for he and his gods had defeated Israel and their God on three separate occasions. And to show off his contempt for Israel's religion he now "commanded that the vessels of gold and of silver that Nebuchadnezzar his father had taken out of the temple in Jerusalem be brought, that the king and his lords, his wives, and his concubines might drink from them."

No previous king of Babylon had shown such contempt for the sacred vessels of a conquered nation. Nebuchadnezzar had placed these vessels in the treasury of his god, with the sacred relics of other nations, and there they had remained ever since. The Babylonians had respected the gods of other nations, though naturally they considered their own to be superior. But not Belshazzar: he would show his disdain for Israel's God by using His vessels as drinking bowls in praise of his own gods of wood and stone!

There were over five thousand of these vessels (5,400, Ezra 1:11), more than enough to serve the guests at Belshazzar's disreputable banquet. "Each of Belshazzar's guests, his thousand lords plus his wives and concubines, had no difficulty in acquiring a handsome vessel with which to continue the bacchanalian festivity" (R.A. Anderson). But the Lord also had an eye on these vessels. He had promised that He would bring them back and restore them to their proper place (Jeremiah 27:19-22), and this in fact was done by the hand of Sheshbazzar (Ezra 1:11).

Belshazzar's profanity was a deliberate insult to a God whom he did not want to know. He was pleased to remember that "Nebuchadnezzar his father had taken (them) out of the temple in Jerusalem", but at the same time he was anxious to forget that Israel's God had humbled his father Nebuchadnezzar, inflicting him with a demeaning mental disorder for seven long years - though all this he knew (5:22). He was also pleased to forget the amazing edict by which Nebuchadnezzar had proclaimed to all peoples, nations, and languages the greatness of the Most High God whom he, Belshazzar, was now despising.

Belshazzar's knowledge and guilt

Belshazzar knew more about Daniel than he was prepared to admit (5:14). F.W. Farrar has written, "He (Belshazzar) must have known of the Rab-mag [Chief magician] Daniel, whose wisdom even as a boy had been found superior to that of all the Chartummim and Ashshaphim; and how his companions had been elevated to supreme satrapies, and how they had been delivered unsinged ... Under no circumstances could such marvels have been forgotten."

Where ignorance prevails the Lord is more than ready to forgive and forget (Luke 23:34; Acts 17:30), but when a heathen king comes face to face with a true believer and prophet he cannot plead ignorance any more. He is now responsible for his actions and attitude and will be called to account for his continued unbelief. Through their contact with Daniel, Nebuchadnezzar and Belshazzar had no excuse for their unbelief. To the one this knowledge became a fragrance from life to life, but to the other a fragrance from death to death (2 Cor. 2:16).

But what was Belshazzar doing holding a feast at all? Already Nabonidus had been defeated at Sippar - on 6 Tishri (10 October 539), according to the Nabonidus Chronicle, only six days before Ugbaru entered Babylon without a battle. The surrounding territory had already been captured; only Babylon remained with its massive walls and fortification. According to Herodotus, Cyrus was a long time in preparing for the siege of Babylon. The Babylonians, already defeated, retreated and shut themselves up in their city.

Belshazzar's feast was an act of defiance and bravado. For him it was business as usual - at least that is what he wanted people to think. He must have regarded the city as impregnable. Herodotus says the outer walls were 87 feet thick and 350 feet high. His figures are thought to be exaggerated, but even so the city may well have seemed impregnable. They had apparently "laid up provisions for many years, and therefore were under no apprehension about a siege" (Herodotus). Evidently Belshazzar had convinced himself, and wished to convince his nobles, that there was no immediate danger: they could hold out for years if it came to a siege.

It was not only the invaders whom Belshazzar was defying. He was defying also the Most High God whom Nebuchadnezzar (his father) had honoured and adored. His desecration of the vessels "was plainly an act of open defiance, calculated to insult the God whose Temple had stood in Jerusalem" (Keil).

The fingers of a human hand appeared

Belshazzar was sitting at one end of the room on a raised dais. On one side of him was a lampstand casting ghostly shadows on the plaster wall. Suddenly a disembodied hand appeared and began to write something on the wall. All Belshazzar's suppressed fears welled up to the surface. He was sure that the writing was a sentence of doom against himself for his licentious lifestyle and his abuse of the sacred vessels from Jerusalem. His face turned white, his hips came loose at the joints, and his knees knocked together. "There is nothing humorous about the description," says Goldingay. "It is a deadly serious comprehensive description of the physical manifestations of terror." (Isaiah 21:3; Nahum 2:10; Ezekiel 21:7; Psalm 69:23.)   Belshazzar's guilty reaction was fully justified. The same divine finger which had inscribed the tablets of stone on Mount Sinai (Exodus 31:18) was now accusing the transgressor. But for some reason which is not explained neither he nor the wise men could read or understand the writing. It has been suggested that the writing was in unfamiliar ideograms (Charles), or simply unpointed Aramaic which was patient of more than one interpretation (or impatient of any).

Wiseman says the writing "has as its most obvious rendering 'mina, mina, shekel and half-shekel (i.e. 60: 60: 1: 1/2 shekel)." If this was the gist of the wise men's thinking, as it is of many modern expositors, their bafflement is understandable, since this line of thinking leads to nothing but confusion.

The third ruler

The reward which Belshazzar offered to the man who could read and interpret the writing included the honour of being third ruler in the kingdom (5:7), and this in fact is what Daniel became, albeit fleetingly (5:29). But why the third ruler? Joseph (Genesis 41:40) and Mordecai (Esther 10:3) were both made second to the king, and Darius planned to set Daniel over the whole kingdom, as his prime minister or second in command (Daniel 6:3).

It is possible that *talti* is simply the title of a high official like its Hebrew equivalent *Shalish* which seems to have lost its numerical content.

Originally the third man on a chariot, it came to denote an officer or captain of high military rank (Exodus 14:7; 1 Kings 9:22 etc.). In this instance, however, it seems likely that "third" is to be understood literally since Belshazzar himself was only second in the kingdom. King Nabonidus (556-539) had entrusted the kingdom to his son Belshazzar while he himself retired to Tema in central Arabia. This he did in the sixth year of his reign (550-549), and it is from this year that Belshazzar's reign is reckoned in Daniel.

According to the Verse Account of Nabonidus, "He entrusted the 'camp' to his eldest (son), the firstborn, the troops everywhere in the country he ordered under his (command). He let (everything) go, entrusted kingship (*sharrutim*) to him ... He turned towards Tema (deep) in the west." (See Wiseman, p.42.)

The highest honour which Belshazzar was able to offer was that of third ruler, and it was this which Daniel received for a few hours in the night of 16 October, 539 BC.

The Queen offers her advice

At this juncture "the Queen" arrives on the scene. No-one knows for certain who this lady was, but there is wide agreement that she was the dowager Queen Mother. It has been surmised that Nabonidus, the absentee king of Babylon, father of Belshazzar, may have married a daughter or wife of Nebuchadnezzar. This would explain why Nebuchadnezzar is repeatedly referred to as Belshazzar's "father" (5:11 three times, 18), in the sense, as so often, of grandfather. Wisemen says, "Nothing is yet known of Nabonidus' wife, so that it is not impossible that she was another daughter of Nebuchadrezzar who married Nabonidus who was already of high rank in Nebuchadrezzar's eighth year" (p.11). Usurpers have frequently sought to legitimize their claim to the throne by marrying a daughter of the previous king, e.g. Herod the Great and Henry VII of England.

The ease and confidence with which she enters the banquet hall unannounced; the deference shown her by the king and nobles; her profound knowledge and respect for Daniel, all suggest that she had been very close to Nebuchadnezzar at the time when Daniel was most influential at court. Her high regard for Daniel, whose understanding and wisdom she commends so strongly, might even suggest that she shared her father's faith in Daniel's God.

Daniel is summoned

Daniel must have been the last person whom Belshazzar wanted to see. But so desperate was his desire to be told the meaning of the writing, and so incapable his wise men to satisfy this desire, that he felt he had no alternative. So Daniel was summoned, now an old man in his eighties, a tall venerable figure with a straight back and flowing white beard. How different from the bloated, red-faced nobles whose terrified eyes stared up at him from every direction!

Daniel politely declined the proffered rewards, not wishing to be beholden in any way to Belshazzar and his court or that anyone should think he was desirous of personal gain. He reminded Belshazzar of "the greatness, glory and majesty" of Nebuchadnezzar his father, a greatness (it is implied) far in excess of anything Belshazzar could lay claim to. But even he, when his heart was lifted up and hardened with pride, "was brought down from his kingly throne and his glory was taken from him." Nebuchadnezzar was abased to such an extent that "his mind was made like that of a beast, and his dwelling was with the wild donkeys. He was fed grass like an ox, and his body was wet with the dew of heaven, until" - yes, there was an until in his case - "until he knew that the Most High God rules the kingdom of mankind and sets over it whom he will."

"But you, Belshazzar," who "knew all this" have not humbled yourself: "you have lifted up yourself against the Lord of heaven." You have compounded your sins by drinking out of "the vessels of his house", and by praising the gods of silver and gold to the neglect of "the God in whose hand is your breath, and whose are all your ways."

These verses, says Leupold, "are the beginning of one of the finest sermons delivered by a court preacher under the most trying circumstances. The preacher is not found remiss in a single item. He tells the whole truth, and tells it with unmistakable clearness. He cringes before no man; he uses no evasion or circumlocution; and he maintains a respectful attitude throughout."

The meaning of the writing

As is usually the case, it is better to be ingenuous than ingenious. In other words, stick closely to the text without reading into it a *double entendre*, a hidden meaning not actually stated and probably not intended.

MENE means "numbered". "God has numbered the days of your kingdom and brought it to an end." Leupold comments, "Here it is the kingdom that is numbered: a count of it, so to say, has been made, and it has been found to equal its total assignment, and so God 'hath determined its destruction'."

TEKEL means "weighed". "You have been weighed in the balances and found wanting." The idea of ones actions or integrity being weighed on the divine scales is frequent in the Bible, e.g. 1 Samuel 2:3; Job 31:6; Psalm 62:9.

(U)PARSIN. The initial U is simply "and". *PARSIN* may be either the plural participle of *PERES* meaning "divided", or more naturally "Persians", in line with *Parsi*, "Persian", in Nehemiah 12:22. Clearly both meanings are intended. Daniel interprets it as if from *PERES*: "Your kingdom is divided (or broken up) and has been given to Media and Persia (*Paras*)."

The fulfilment

It was that very night that Belshazzar was killed. In Herodotus' account, Cyrus "having diverted the river by means of a canal, into the lake, which was before the swamp, he made the ancient channel fordable by the sinking of the river." He ordered his army to enter the city as soon as the stream was fordable. Although this ruse is not mentioned in the cuneiform sources, it is nevertheless "entirely possible" (Goldingay). In any case Belshazzar's trust in his fortifications proved misplaced.

According to Herodotus again, "those of the Babylonians who inhabited the centre knew nothing of the capture (for it happened to be a festival); but they were dancing at the time, and enjoying themselves, till they received certain information of the truth. And thus was Babylon taken for the first time."

Daniel Six

The Devil like a Roaring Lion

It was remarked in chapter 3 that much light is thrown on the historical portions of Daniel, chapters 3 and 6 in particular, if Daniel is treated as a type of Christ, and his friends, Shadrach, Meshach and Abednego, as types of Christian believers. In the same way as the fiery furnace speaks of the fires of persecution, the den of lions speaks emphatically of the Devil and his minions (1 Peter 5:8). In Daniel 6 we find an elaborate prefigurement of the death and resurrection of Christ, probably more complete than anywhere else in the Old Testament. The following are some of the parallels which come to mind.

The king planned to set him over the whole kingdom

Daniel 6:3: "Then this Daniel became distinguished above all the other presidents and satraps, because an excellent spirit was in him. And the king planned to set him over the whole kingdom."

His praises are acclaimed even more superlatively in 5:12 in the words of the Queen Mother: "an excellent spirit, knowledge, and understanding to interpret dreams, and solve problems were found in this Daniel." And by Belshazzar himself: "I have heard of you that the spirit of the gods is in you, and that light and understanding and excellent wisdom are found in you" (5:14). E.J. Young truly remarks, "An honest man of conviction in the midst of government or ecclesiastical politicians stands out like a fair flower in a barren wilderness." Such a man was Daniel among the ruling junta of Babylon.

All these virtues shine with a more brilliant lustre in Him who is "the radiance of the glory of God and the exact imprint of His nature," who became "as much superior to angels as the name he has inherited is more excellent than theirs" (Hebrews 1:3-4).

As for God's plan to set Christ over the whole kingdom we need look no further than the words of Gabriel to the virgin Mary: "He will be great and will be called the Son of the Most High. And the Lord God will give to him the throne of his father David, and he will reign over the house of Jacob for ever, and of his kingdom there will be no end" (Luke 1:32-33). The title "Most High" also reminds us of Daniel where God is so called thirteen times in the Aramaic portion.

No fault was found in him

Daniel 6:4: "Then the presidents and the satraps sought to find a ground for complaint against Daniel with regard to the kingdom, but they could find no ground for complaint or any fault, because he was faithful, and no error or fault was found in him."

With this compare Matthew 26:59-60, "Now the chief priests and the whole Council were seeking false testimony against Jesus that they might put him to death, but they found none, though many false witnesses came forward." 1 Peter 2:22-23, "He committed no sin, neither was deceit found in his mouth. When he was reviled, he did not revile in return; when he suffered, he did not threaten, but continued entrusting himself to him who judges justly." See also Isaiah 53:9; 2 Corinthians 5:21; Hebrews 4:15; 7:26; 1 John 3:5.

The law of his god was the only ground for complaint

Daniel 6:5: "Then these men said, 'We shall not find any ground for complaint against this Daniel unless we find it in connection with the law of his God'."

This was also the only ground for accusing Jesus: Mark 14:61-64, "Again the high priest asked him, 'Are you the Christ, the Son of the Blessed?' And Jesus said, 'I am ...' And the high priest tore his garments and said, 'What further witnesses do we need? You have heard his blasphemy.'"

They came by agreement

Daniel 6:6: "Then these presidents and satraps came by agreement to the king."

This they were doing repeatedly, 6:12,15. The same verb is found in Psalm 2:1, "Why do the nations *rage* and the peoples plot in vain?" And the noun in Psalm 64:2, "Hide me from the secret plots of the wicked, from the *throng* of evildoers"; and Psalm 55:14, "within God's house we walked in the *throng*." The word includes the ideas of agreement, conspiracy, unlawful assembly, and the forceful pressing of charges.

Goldingay notes "a series of motifs parallel to Psalm 2". "Heathen rulers have mustered and devised their plot, but God has acted on behalf of his servant, giving him the power to have them torn to pieces, to rule over their realm, and to compel them to serve God with trembling fear."

Darius their only king

Daniel 6:6: "O King Darius, live for ever!"

Their allegiance was one of convenience and self-interest, as was that of the chief priests in John 19:15, "The chief priests answered, 'We have no king but Caesar.'"

"Suspecting nothing, pleased with the flattery of the decree, glad to have such obsequious nobles, the king affixes his signature" (Leupold). This however was not true of Pilate, Caesar's representative. He suspected everything and was far from pleased; he nevertheless affixed his signature!

Daniel acted as he had done previously

Daniel 6:10: "When Daniel knew that the document had been signed, he went to his house where he had windows in his upper chamber open towards Jerusalem. He got down on his knees three times a day and prayed and gave thanks before his God, as he had done previously."

Jesus did the same: Luke 22:39, "And he came out and went, as was his custom, to the Mount of Olives," and there He prayed three times (Matthew 26:44). The gist of our Lord's Prayer was this, "Father, if you are willing, remove this cup from me. Nevertheless, not my will, but yours, be done" (Luke 22:42). It would surprise me if Daniel's prayer was not in essence the same. The Mount of Olives, we are told, was "opposite the temple", Mark 13:3.

Daniel was only following Solomon's instructions in his great dedicatory prayer. Solomon here anticipates the possibility that Israel will be carried away captive to the land of the enemy, and prays, "if they repent with all their mind and all their heart in the land of their enemies, who carried them captive, and pray to you towards their land, which you gave to their fathers, the city that you have chosen, and the house that I have built for your name, then hear in heaven your dwelling place their prayer and their plea, and maintain their cause ..." (1 Kings 8:48-49). Daniel did as he was told and his prayer was answered.

Daniel is accused

Daniel 6:13: "Daniel, who is one of the exiles from Judah, pays no attention to you, O king, or the injunction you have signed, but makes his petition three times a day."

They tried to portray Daniel as a foreign turncoat who was now showing his true colours by disloyalty to the king. The whole company of elders and chief priests went to Pilate with a similar charge, "We found this man misleading our nation and forbidding us to give tribute to Caesar, and saying that he himself is Christ, a king" (Luke 23:2).

They accuse Him of sedition (forbidding to pay tribute), treason (claiming to be king himself), affray or incitement to public disorder ("He stirs up the people", 23:5). Daniel is accused of contempt for the king, infraction of the king's order, and civil disobedience.

Goldingay says, "every word they speak, as well as every move they make, concerns intrigue, manipulation, treachery, duplicity and scheming. They have the arrogant boldness of a crowd bolstered up by each other into bravado and folly." It was the same with those who accused our Lord, and for both groups what lay behind it was jealousy (Matthew 27:18; Daniel 6:3-4).

Darius laboured to rescue him

Daniel 6:14: "Then the king, when he heard these words, was much distressed and set his mind to deliver Daniel. And he laboured till the sun went down to rescue him."

Pilate likewise did his best to release Jesus. John 19:12, "From then on Pilate sought to release him, but the Jews cried out, 'If you release this man, you are not Caesar's friend'"; Luke 23:15,16,22, "I have found in him no guilt deserving death. I will therefore punish and release him."

Campbell observes, "Nebuchadnezzar, the autocrat, tried to kill God's three servants, but could not: Darius, the democrat, tried to save God's servant, but could not. God saved them all!" Pilate, who had the power of life and death, tried to save Jesus, but could not. God raised Him from the dead!

The law of the Medes and Persians

Daniel 6:15: "Know, O king, that it is a law of the Medes and Persians that no injunction or ordinance that the king establishes can be changed."

There are two laws mentioned in this story: the law of the Medes and Persians and the law of Daniel's God (v.5). There was also another 'law' in contention: the law of the scheming rulers. The presidents and satraps were in the same dilemma as the high priests and elders. On the one hand they had a 'law' by which Daniel ought to die; on the other hand they had no power to impose the death penalty. In order to get their own way, the presidents and satraps had to manipulate the law of the State so as to silence the law of God. The law of the State is forced to comply contrary to its own ethos and better judgment, unable to stand against the lies and persistence of unlawful men.

It is the same in the Gospel story. John 18:31, "Pilate said to them, 'Take him yourself and judge him by your own law.' The Jews said to him, 'It is not lawful for us to put anyone to death'."

Daniel is thrown to the lions

Daniel 6:16: "Then the king commanded, and Daniel was brought and cast into the den of lions. The king declared to Daniel, 'May your God, whom you serve continually, deliver you!'"

There is nothing improbable about Daniel being cast into a den of lions. As Wiseman points out, "lions from cages were hunted, as a trial of royal prowess, in the *ambassu* or royal parklands from the days of Tiglathpileser I onwards." The word translated "den" means "pit" or "cistern". It has generally been supposed that the pit had an opening at the top for throwing in meat and for light, and a side entrance for the convenience of the keepers and to let out the lions.

There are not a few references to lions, chiefly in the Psalms where they are indicative of life-threatening situations. What was literal for Daniel was generic for others, including our Lord whose sufferings are anticipated in the Psalms. This is particularly true of Psalm 22 which says (v.13), "They open wide their mouths at me, like a ravening and roaring lion"; and verse 21, "Save me from the mouth of the lion." See also Psalm 35:17; 91:11-13; 1 Peter 5:8; 2 Timothy 4:17. It is especially the devil who is compared to a roaring lion. He overreached himself in the crucifixion of Christ and sealed his own fate in the process (Hebrews 2:14)!

The last clause of Daniel 6:16 is translated in the *KJV*, "Thy God, whom thou servest continually, he will deliver thee." If this is correct, it constitutes "one of the most remarkable confessions of faith that ever came from the mouth of a heathen monarch" (A.E. Knoch). Most commentators think that "may he deliver you" is most probably the intended meaning, while admitting that the *KJV* is what it actually says:

imperfect rather than jussive.

Darius against all hope believed in hope that Daniel would be delivered. He may have been familiar with the story of Shadrach, Meshach and Abednego which would have entered Babylonian folklore.

A stone was brought ... and sealed

Daniel 6:17: "And a stone was brought and laid on the mouth of the den, and the king sealed it with his own signet and with the signet of his lords, that nothing might be changed concerning Daniel."

Almost every detail of this story finds an answering chord in the narrative of the crucifixion and resurrection of Christ. The placing of a stone across the entrance of the den, that stone being sealed, is precisely what was done at the garden tomb. Matthew 27:60, "And he (Joseph of Arithmathea) rolled a great stone to the entrance of the tomb and went away"; verses 65-66, "Pilate said to them, 'You have a guard of soldiers. Go, make it as secure as you can. So they went and made the tomb secure by sealing the stone and setting a guard."

William Hendriksen comments, "In the presence of these soldiers who have been ordered to keep this tomb under their surveillance, so that no one will tamper with it, a cord covered with clay or wax on which an official seal has been impressed is affixed to the stone at the grave's entrance. Surely, no one will dare to break this seal or to move this stone."

This is precisely what Darius did on the great stone he had laid over the lion's den.

Darius went in haste to the den

Daniel 6:19: "Then, at break of day (lit. "at dawn when the sun rose"), the king arose and went in haste to the den of lions."

Darius forsakes his role as head of State and takes his place alongside the humble believer whose whole being is in turmoil having lost the anchor of his soul. He did precisely what Mary Magdalene and the other women did at early dawn on the first day of the week. Matthew 28:1, "Now after the Sabbath, towards the dawn of the first day of the week, Mary Magdalene and the other Mary went to see the tomb." Luke 24:1; John 20:1.

The king was exceedingly glad

Daniel 6:23: "Then the king was exceedingly glad, and commanded that Daniel be taken up out of the den."

Darius' reaction at hearing that Daniel was alive was the same as that of the women and the disciples. Matthew 28:8, "So they departed quickly from the tomb with fear and great joy."

Whereas Nebuchadnezzar had been astonished (startled, alarmed) to see four men walking unbound in the midst of the fire (3:24-25), Darius was simply overjoyed. He was, it seems, half expecting Daniel to be alive. He would hardly have gone to the den so early in the morning without a strong premonition that Daniel's God could deliver, and probably had delivered, His servant.

Again, it has been questioned whether Darius was a truly converted man. Leupold, as might be expected from his disparaging remarks about Nebuchadnezzar, is dismissive of any suggestion that Darius was truly converted. More to the point is Goldingay's comment: "It might be possible to make these affirmations [in verses 26-29] without being 'converted'... but this is to miss the point of Darius' confession at the end of the story. The confession goes far beyond that at the end of chap. 3 in acknowledging the living, enduring, secure and active power of Daniel's God." It is in fact far closer to Nebuchadnezzar's confession at the end of chap. 4.

It is indeed remarkable that so many of those kings, Nebuchadnezzar, Darius and Cyrus in particular, were so well disposed towards the God of Israel. For this providential situation they had, humanly speaking, only Daniel to thank.

Daniel's accusers thrown to the lions

Daniel 6:24: "And the king commanded, and those men who had maliciously accused Daniel were brought and cast into the den of lions - they, their children, and their wives."

With this we may compare Matthew 27:25, "And all the people answered, 'His blood be on us and on our children!'" And so it happened in AD 70. The Law of Moses would have spared the women and children (Deuteronomy 24:16; 2 Kings 14:6). But in a few cases, such as Korah and his associates (Numbers 16:32) and Achan (Joshua 7:24), whole households were punished. It must be assumed in these cases that the whole family was implicated in the crime in question.

The word translated "maliciously accused", here and in 3:8, is literally "ate the pieces". With wry humour it is now the turn of the lions to eat the pieces of Daniel's accusers! Their fate is described in the next verse, "before they reached the bottom of the den, the lions overpowered them and broke all their bones in pieces."

A new decree: Daniel's God to be feared and honoured

Daniel 6:25-27: "Then King Darius wrote to all the peoples, nations, and languages that dwell in all the earth: Peace be multiplied to you. I make a decree, that in all my royal dominion people are to tremble and fear before the God of Daniel ... he who has saved Daniel from the power of the lions."

With this we might compare the apostle Paul's proclamation to the Athenian Gentiles in Acts 17:30-31, "The times of ignorance God overlooked, but now he commands all people everywhere to repent, because he has fixed a day on which he will judge the world in righteousness by a man whom he has appointed; and of this he has given assurance to all by raising him from the dead."

Daniel's miraculous deliverance had changed the situation completely. Everyone must now recognise and fear Daniel's all-powerful God because He had proved His pre-eminence in such a remarkable way by saving Daniel from the power of the lions. Even more decisively the resurrection of Christ has changed the situation completely. All people everywhere are now commanded to repent, because God will judge the world by the Man whom He has appointed. Of this He has given us proof and assurance in that He raised Him from the dead.

Daniel 6 is the story of two decrees: the 'irrevocable' decree pronouncing death on the transgressor, and the enduring decree that all men should tremble and fear before the God of Daniel. Paul also speaks of two laws, one leading to condemnation and death ("the law of sin and death") and the other leading to acquittal and life ("the law of the Spirit of life", Romans 8:2). The king's unchangeable law was in tatters when it condemned to death a completely innocent man and then proved itself incapable of executing him. So also is the law of sin and death in tatters since the resurrection of Christ.

By His death on the cross Christ has abolished the law of commandments and ordinances (Ephesians 2:15), cancelled the record of debt that stood against us with its legal demands (Colossians 2:14). This He set aside, nailing it to the cross. The only law which applies now is the law of the Spirit of life which operates through repentance from dead works and faith in the One whom God raised from the dead.

Daniel Seven

Four Marine Monsters

Daniel 7 is the last of the chapters written in Aramaic. The subject matter is "four kings who shall arise out of the earth", here depicted as four great beasts (v.17). In the structure of Daniel this chapter corresponds to the second where also four Gentile kingdoms are described. But it does not follow from this that the four kingdoms of chapter 7 are necessarily the same as those of chapter 2. Each prophecy in Daniel is an advance on that which precedes. It takes up some feature of what has already been revealed, enlarges on it, and adds additional material until, by the end of the book, the picture is complete.

The identity of the four kingdoms in chapters 2 and 7 has been accepted as beyond dispute, or simply taken for granted, by the majority of commentators. By several Luther's words are quoted: "In this interpretation and opinion all the world are agreed, and history and fact abundantly establish it." In the words of Walvoord, "the prevailing opinion of orthodoxy has always held this position [especially that Rome is the fourth kingdom] since the early church." But the agreement of orthodoxy with the world does not inspire much confidence in the correctness of the view expressed! Still less is confirmation by history a convincing reason, since Daniel's visions need to be viewed *prospectively* from Daniel's standpoint, not *retrospectively* from that of "history and fact". Agreement, all too often, is agreement in error. It should provoke caution, even suspicion, rather than uncritical acceptance.

The four kingdoms contemporaneous

The first writer to question the traditional interpretation, albeit tentatively, was Sir Robert Anderson toward the end of the nineteenth century. In his book *The Coming Prince* (pp. 274-77) he gives seven reasons why this interpretation falls short of conviction. His arguments were taken up and enlarged upon by G.H. Lang in 1950 (pp.77-81).

Reasons for thinking that the four kingdoms should be viewed as contemporary/ future rather than consecutive/ historical are as follows:

(1) "Repetition is rare in Scripture." It would be surprising if this chapter were simply to repeat what had already been revealed and explained in chapter 2.

(2) Daniel had his dream in the first year of Belshazzar (7:1). "How then could the rise of that empire be the subject of the prophecy?" For so it is presented in verse 17.

(3) "In the history of Babylonia there is nothing to correspond with the predicted course of the first beast, for it is scarcely legitimate to suppose that the vision was a prophecy about Nebuchadnezzar" - whose death had already occurred.

(4) "At its advent the leopard had four wings and four heads. This was its primary and normal condition, and it was in this condition that 'dominion was given to it'." But in Daniel 8:8,22 and 11:4 the division into four is only apparent after the great horn (= the first king) has been broken.

(5) "Verse 3 seems to imply that the four beasts came up together, and at all events there is nothing to suggest a series of empires, each destroying its predecessor." As Lang observes, "The four winds breaking forth together from all quarters signifies a general commotion arising in all directions simultaneously." A rather similar situation, except in reverse, is portrayed in Revelation 7:1. There the four winds are held in abeyance pending the sealing of the 144,000 from the twelve tribes of Israel.

(6) When the fourth beast is destroyed, the others continue for a while: "their dominion was taken away, but their lives were prolonged for a season and a time" (v.12). The only natural understanding of this statement is that all four beasts were existing concurrently. Commentators like to compare 2:35 where "the iron, the clay, the bronze, the silver, and the gold, all together were broken in pieces." Here the entire image is destroyed at one blow because each successive empire

embraced the domains of its predecessor, so that at the end the image is still standing in its original integrity. But in 7:12 the situation is quite different. Here the four beasts are not destroyed at one and the same time. Only one is destroyed and the other three permitted to continue. Nor do their territories overlap. Only the fourth beast corresponds to the fourth kingdom of Daniel 2; the other three beasts occupy different domains altogether.

William Campbell correctly observes, "The first three beasts are contemporary with the fourth; and the fourth is contemporary with the Second Coming of Christ (v.11, 17-22). Therefore, the time-setting of the whole chapter is in the last days of this age."

Lucas admits, "The prolongation of the 'lives' of the first three beasts after their loss of dominion is a source of puzzlement to commentators." When commentators try to impose on a passage an interpretation that does not fit, the result is bound to be puzzlement. Lucas observes quite correctly that "God's judgment is discriminating and just. The fourth beast was different from the others and so was dealt with differently, as its greater offences deserved." That is true, but it offers no relief to the puzzlement which the traditional interpretation gives rise to.

The interpretation which commends itself is that all four kings (or kingdoms) will rise at the same time as the result of an international upheaval such as has occurred twice in the twentieth century.

What Daniel saw

There is a phrase which occurs nine times in this chapter, *hazeh haweth*, "I was beholding", or better "as I was looking" (vs.2,4,6,7,9,11 bis,13,21). It also occurs four times in chapters 2 and 4 of what Nebuchadnezzar was seeing. Chapter 7 is all about what Daniel was seeing in his night vision in the first year of Belshazzar. The date is reckoned to be 550 BC, more than fifty years after Nebuchadnezzar's dream of the Great Image in the second year of his reign (603/2 BC) and eleven years before the fall of Babylon in 539 BC.

What Daniel saw was the four winds of heaven churning up the great sea, as a result of which he saw four hybrid monsters rise out of the sea, all of them very different. The turbulence of the sea represents the strife of nations as in Isaiah 17:12-13; 57:20 and Jeremiah 6:23. The hybrid monsters are symbolic of "four kings who shall arise out of the earth" (Daniel 7:17), hence the great sea stands for the land mass from which they arise. The four monsters rise from the sea one after the other, but "this in itself hardly excludes the possibility of understanding the kings they represent as contemporaneous" (Goldingay).

The Great Sea

Lang makes much of the fact that "the great sea", in all its occurrences, invariably signifies the Mediterranean. "It is clear", he says, "that from the time of Moses the term had one regular meaning, and that this was still current in Daniel's day, as witnessed by its use by his contemporary, Ezekiel." He refers to Ezekiel 48:28. Lang continues, "it is of great importance to retain the normal, literal sense of 'the great sea' because it fixes the exact area of the disturbance whenever it shall come. The four beasts are to arise in the Mediterranean area; they 'came up from the sea,' the Great Sea just mentioned." He then makes the point that neither Babylon nor Medo-Persia arose from the Mediterranean area.

But this argument lacks credibility. Granted that the Great Sea stands for the Mediterranean, what Daniel saw was four beasts coming out of the Mediterranean. That is the vision; the interpretation is given in verse 17: "These four great beasts are four kings who shall arise *out of the earth*." So the four beasts stand for four kings and the Mediterranean stands for the earth. As so often, the tempestuous sea stands for the clash and frenzy of nations. Out of one such clash these four kings will arise, but they will rise from the earth as a whole, not necessarily from the Mediterranean area.

The first monster

The first beast he saw was like a lion with eagles' wings. The picture is one of great strength coupled with swiftness of movement. Saul and Jonathan were "swifter than eagles" and "stronger than lions", according to 2 Samuel 1:23. Nebuchadnezzar is referred to as a lion (Jeremiah 4:7; 50:17), and his armies as eagles (Ezekiel 17:3), but "neither has a distinctive association with Babylon or with Nebuchadnezzar" (Goldingay). Any nation or person with lion-like qualities can be so described: Judah (Genesis 49:9), Dan (Deuteronomy 33:22), the Gadites (1 Chronicles 12:8), David's pursuers (Psalm 7:2), the wicked (Psalm 10:9; 17:12; Proverbs 28:15), the prophets (Ezekiel 22:25), the locust nation (Joel 1:6), the remnant of Jacob (Micah 5:8), Nineveh (Nahum 2:11-12), the king of Assyria (Jeremiah 50:17), Jerusalem's officials (Zephaniah 3:3).

As Daniel looked, its wings were plucked off. It was also raised from the ground and made to stand on two feet like a man, and a man's mind was given to it. This is commonly referred to Nebuchadnezzar, but he had died twelve years before and his recovery from madness some years before that. The mind of a man was given to this creature (7:4), but to Nebuchadnezzar the mind of a beast (4:16). Daniel's vision is not about the past; it relates to four kings who *shall* arise out of the earth (v.17). The king or kingdom referred to loses its eagle-like qualities (speed and greed), and is enabled to think and behave like a rational human being.

The second monster

The second creature was like a bear, raised up on one side. It had three ribs in its mouth and it was told, "Arise, devour much flesh." The bear is second only to the lion in strength and ferocity (1 Samuel 17:34-37; Amos 5:19; Proverbs 28:15). According to Proverbs 28:15, "Like a roaring lion or a charging bear is a wicked ruler over a poor people." Though ponderous and slow the bear is nonetheless a formidable foe when hungry or roused.

The bear was seen as raised up on one side, a feature which has perplexed commentators. On the strength of the demi-couchant bull in Babylonian and Persian art, Montgomery supposes that the two legs on the near side are raised as though the animal were rising. "The animal then is pausing to devour a mouthful before springing again on its prey, to which feat an oracular voice encourages it." In addition, it had three ribs in its mouth. These are often said to be Babylon, Lydia and Egypt by those who understand the bear to signify Medo-Persia. But as Leupold observes, "Such enumerations of three powers are more or less arbitrary."

The third monster

The third beast had the appearance of a leopard with the four wings of a bird on its back. It also had four heads and dominion was given it. The leopard is another dangerous predator, associated with the lion and bear in Hosea 13:7-8, famed for its speed (Habakkuk 1:8), cunning and stealth of attack (Jeremiah 5:6; Hosea 13:7). "No excess fat adorns a leopard, just rippling muscle and flashing speed. Leopards have been clocked at over seventy miles per hour" (Ron Cantrell). This amazing speed is increased fourfold by its having the four wings of a bird. It has in addition four heads, denoting perhaps four dominions or regions.

According to Lang, "The third beast will be as attractive and as cruel as a leopard, and as swift as a four-winged bird. It will also have a fourfold government, probably being a confederacy of four powers." Its four heads are referred to in the same way as its four wings ("to it four wings ... and four heads to the beast"). That is how it was at its first appearance, not twenty years after its demise as in the case of Alexander's empire.

The fourth monster

No creature comes to mind when the fourth beast is described. It was simply more terrifying, dreadful, and powerful than any wild animal in existence. It was moreover quite different from all the beasts that were before it (7:7). The word translated "before it" means "in its presence" as elsewhere in Daniel 2-7 (42 times). There is no instance where it means before in point of time. This beast had great iron teeth with which it tore and devoured its prey, and claws of bronze (v.19). It had ten horns as well. "The beast is simply itself - a beast, a generic horror, predatory, exceeding all, forebears, descendants, peers, in quality and scope of malevolence" (Berrigan).

This beast at least can be identified. It is the same as the iron kingdom of Daniel 2. Its iron teeth, its great strength, its terrifying ability to break and to crush, and its ten horns, proves this to be true. The ten horns correspond to the ten toes of the image. The toes are mentioned in 2:41-42, and their number, ten, follows from the fact that the image is in the form of a man. (For the same reason we know there were two arms, two legs, and two feet, though the text does not actually say so!) It is the fourth kingdom especially in its final and most deadly phase that is before us, when the little horn, the Antichrist, rises from among the ten and uproots three of them.

The little horn

Of this horn we are told three things in verses 8 and 20, and another four things in verses 21 and 25.

(1) He will have eyes like the eyes of a man. He will be a man of unusual intelligence, alertness, foresight and perspicacity. The eyes also speak of arrogance and disdain (Proverbs 30:13,17 etc.), haughtiness (Proverbs 21:4; Isaiah 2:11), insatiable desire (Proverbs 27:20), and pitiless cruelty (Isaiah 13:18). "All commanding personalities have notable eyes, revealing discernment and penetrating insight into men and affairs" (Lang).

(2) He will have a mouth speaking great things. Exactly the same words are applied to the beast out of the sea in Revelation 13: "a mouth speaking great things and blasphemies" (v.5, *KJV*). This beast is an embodiment of all the beasts of Daniel 7. Its appearance is that of a leopard with bear's feet and a lion's mouth. It has also ten horns and seven heads, the same as the total number of heads of Daniel's four beasts. This is what he will become at the height of his power: the voice, mind, magnet, and idol of the greater part of the world. In Isaiah 10:12-14 the boastful looks of the king of Assyria are accompanied by arrogant words: "By the strength of my hand I have done it, and by my wisdom, for I have understanding ..." This man will be an orator and demagogue, "with that hypnotic energy which carries the crowd with it and moves masses of men to obey and co-operate" (Lang).

(3) He will seem greater than his fellows (v.20). He will stand out from among his contemporaries, an impressive figure of a man. Writing in 1950 Lang affirmed, "Of recent years Europe was familiar

with portraits of just such men as Antichrist will be - proud, stern, resolute, despotic, yet fascinating."

(4) He will make war with the saints (the faithful in Israel) and prevail over them (v.21). Again exactly the same words are used of the beast that ascends out of the abyss in Revelation 11:7 and 13:7. According to verse 25, he will wear out the saints of the Most High. The verb "wear out" is applied to sacks, wineskins and sandals in Joshua 9:4-5 and frequently to garments (e.g. Deuteronomy 8:4). It will be a war of attrition by which the saints are denied the basic necessities of life, making their very existence intolerable if not impossible. The temptation to receive the mark of the beast will be overwhelming, but to do so will be fatal (Revelation 14:9-10).

(5) He will speak words against the Most High (v.25). In 11:36 it is said of the "contemptible" king of the North, "He shall exalt himself and magnify himself above every god, and he shall speak astonishing things against the God of gods." According to 2 Thessalonians 2:4 he "opposes and exalts himself against every so-called god or object of worship, so that he takes his seat in the temple of God, proclaiming himself to be God." His astonishing words will be blasphemies of the most outspoken and outrageous kind, but his words will be enthusiastically received by the majority of mankind who will revel in his profanity.

(6) He will think to change the times and the law (or "times and law"). Exactly what he will try to change is not revealed, but it will probably be the God-given rules which underpin our social order: marriage, family life, the working-week. He may try to impose a decimal regime on every aspect of life as was tried in the French Revolution with disastrous results, and he will certainly dismantle the laws and festivals of the Jews as part of his harassment of the people of the saints. G.H. Lang writes:

> He will study to organize mankind in every affair upon a new basis under new arrangements, which will be designed to banish the remembrance of the past and to usher in an entirely new order and era, and for the time allotted he will succeed; "they shall be given

into his hand." It can be easily conceived that mankind, utterly wearied by the complete failure of all previous civilizations and arrangements, will be ready for the new experiment and will accept the changes gladly. An effect of the scheme will be to make illegal the whole divine programme of the Jewish year, its time of commencement, sabbaths, months, seasonal feasts, and all else that, from its institution and ever since, has severed Israel's national life and routine from that of every people. This was its design, and this Antichrist will seek to reverse it in the interests of his programme of the unity of the world under himself. That "very small remnant" of Israel (Isaiah 1:9; Joel 2:15-17, etc.) that will be turned by Elijah unto Jehovah and will be remembering and doing the Law of Moses (Malachi 4:4-6; Revelation 11:1-13), will be indeed hard pressed by this measure. The endeavour to follow the old religious seasons and law will throw them out of gear with the whole world machinery, and will expose them to the full penalty of the criminal laws of the empire. (pp. 90 f.)

(7) The saints will be given into his hand for a time, times and half a time. This is the length of time he is allowed for "the shattering of the power of the holy people" (12:7). It is generally accepted that three and a half times are meant, the word "times" being dual in meaning if not in form, and that a "time" is equivalent to a year. In Revelation 12:6 and 14 the length of time the Woman is nourished in the wilderness is 1260 days in verse 6 (that is, three and a half years of 360 days), and a time, times and half a time in verse 14. The two periods are synonymous. Here also we have another link with the beast of Revelation 13, for that beast "was allowed to exercise authority for 42 months" (13:5), 42 months being the same as 1260 days. Time, times and half a time, 1260 days and 42 months are simply different ways of speaking of the same period of time, which turns out to be the second half-seven of the last seven years of Daniel's Seventy Sevens as revealed in Daniel 9.

This interpretation is confirmed by Montgomery who certainly had no sympathy for a futurist or premillennial understanding of prophecy. He writes:

Essaying an exact interpretation, 'time' may be interpreted as 'year' after the usual interpretation of 4:13 [English 4:16]. The traditional and by far the most common understanding of 'times' is as of a dual; the word is pointed as a plural, but the Aramaic later having lost the dual, the tendency of M [the Massoretic Text] is to ignore it in Biblical Aramaic (see Note on 'eyes,' v.8). Accordingly $1 + 2 + \frac{1}{2} = 3\frac{1}{2}$ years. This term is identical with the half-year week of $9:27 = 3\frac{1}{2}$ years ... This interpretation of our passage was fixed in the 1st cent. A.D., for in connection with the citation of it in Revelation 12:14 the apocalyptist interprets it as meaning 42 months, 11:2, 13:5, and 1,260 days, 11:3.

Will his authority be universal?

The fourth kingdom will devour the whole earth, trample it down and break it in pieces (7:23). Will, therefore, the fourth kingdom be universal in extent? This cannot be argued from the expression "the whole earth" (*kol ha-'arets*, all the earth), as Lang does for example (pp.192-93), since the extent of the land intended by this expression depends entirely on the context.

It can refer to so small an area as a threshing-floor (Judges 6:37-40 "all the ground"), to a battlefield (2 Samuel 18:8 "all the country"), or to a much larger area such as the extent of the famine in the days of Joseph (Genesis 41:57; 47:13). It can refer to the whole land of Egypt, Canaan, Uz, Judah, Babylon etc., or the terrain covered by the he-goat (Daniel 8:5). It can also mean the entire earth, either actually or potentially, as required by the context.

Both Nebuchadnezzar and Darius claimed dominion over all the earth (Daniel 4:1; 6:25), but this was not literally true. Nebuchadnezzar's authority did not literally extend to the ends of the whole earth any more than it reached to heaven (4:20,22). But in the case of the Antichrist there is reason to believe that his influence really will be universal. It is said of the first beast in Revelation 13 that "authority was given it over every tribe and people and language and nation, and all who dwell on earth will worship it, everyone whose name has not been written before the foundation of the world in the book of life of the Lamb that was slain" (13:7-8). Likewise it is said of the "eternal gospel" that it will be proclaimed "to those who dwell on the earth, to every nation and tribe and language and people" (14:6). And of the one like a Son of Man that "to him was given dominion and glory and a kingdom, that all peoples, nations and languages should serve him" (Daniel 7:14). It would certainly appear that the influence of the Antichrist, at the height of his power (conferred and controlled by Satan, Revelation 13:2-4), will be universal as universal as can be. In a world unified both politically and economically, his demonic influence will be felt in every country of the world, though the actual dominion he controls will be of limited extent.

The judgment scene

The judgment scene which follows (7:9-10) may be compared with those in Revelation 4-5 and 20:11-12. In each case a throne is placed and the majestic figure of God Almighty takes His seat. He is surrounded by thousands upon thousands, indeed myriads of angels (Revelation 5:11), and the books are opened (20:12). The Ancient of Days (vs. 9,13,22), who is seated on the throne, is not simply One who is advanced in years. He is God "from everlasting to everlasting", to whom a thousand years are as a watch in the night (Psalm 90:1-4). Campbell aptly compares Job 12:12, "With the ancient is wisdom; in length of days understanding."

He is the One who takes His seat on the throne and pronounces judgment on the four monsters. The fourth monster was killed, its body destroyed and committed to the flames. The other beasts had their dominion taken away, but their lives were prolonged for a short period ("a season and a time").

The everlasting kingdom

We come finally to the last kingdom of all, that associated with "One like a son of man". He comes with the clouds and is presented before the Ancient of Days. "And to him was given dominion and glory and a kingdom, that all peoples, nations and languages should serve him. His dominion is an everlasting dominion, which shall not pass away, and his kingdom one that shall not be destroyed" (v.14).

Here we have the kingdom that the God of heaven will set up, "a kingdom that shall never be destroyed, nor shall the kingdom be left to another people" (2:44). Both Nebuchadnezzar and Darius claimed authority over "all peoples, nations and languages" (3:4,29; 4:1; 5:19; 6:25), but only God's rule can lay claim to universal extent and everlasting permanence (2:44; 4:3,34; 6:26; 7:14).

This kingdom He shares with "the people of the saints of the Most High". Having been gored so terribly by the little horn, the saints are now rewarded for their steadfastness. They are given "the kingdom and the dominion and the greatness of the kingdoms under the whole heaven ... His kingdom will be an everlasting kingdom, and all rulers will worship and obey him" (v.27 *NIV*).

One like unto a son of man

But who is the One like a son of man, to whom was given dominion and glory and a kingdom? The expression itself (*ke-bar 'enash*) simply means one like a human being. Its Hebrew equivalent, *ben 'enosh*, is to be found in Psalm 144:3 where it is paired with *'adam*, man: "O Lord, what is man that you regard him, or the son of man that you think of him? Man is like a breath; his days are like a passing shadow." The plural of the same expression in Aramaic occurs in Daniel 2:38 and 5:21. In 5:21 "driven from among the children of mankind" is the equivalent of "driven from among men" in 4:25.

The more usual expression, with the same meaning, is *ben 'adam*, son of man or child of Adam. It occurs quite frequently in the singular, usually in a pejorative sense, e.g. Job 25:6, "how much less man, *'enosh*, who is a maggot, and the son of man, who is a worm!"; Isaiah 51:12, "who are you that you are afraid of man who dies, of the son of man who is made like grass?" Ezekiel is called "son of man" around ninety times and Daniel himself once (8:17).

The most important passage where "son of man" occurs is undoubtedly Psalm 8, to which Daniel 7:14 seems to allude. It says there:

What is man (*'enosh*) that you are mindful of him,

and the son of man that you care for him?
Yet you have made him a little lower than the heavenly beings
and crowned him with glory and honour.
You have given him dominion over the works of your hands;
you have put all things under his feet,
all sheep and oxen, and also the beasts of the field,
the birds of the heavens, and the fish of the sea,
whatever passes along the paths of the seas.

This passage in context refers to mankind, the race of men, as in Genesis 1:26 on which it is based. But in Hebrews 2 it is quoted with reference to Jesus, "who for a little while was made lower than the angels," but now is "crowned with glory and honour because of the suffering of death" (2:9). The question which exercises scholars today is whether the One like a son of man in Daniel 7:14 is personal or collective. That is, does it refer exclusively to Christ or is it synonymous with "the people of the saints of the Most High" in verse 27?

In Revelation 1:13 the "One like a son of man" in the midst of the lampstands is the exalted Lord Jesus, but that in itself does not prove that Daniel speaks exclusively of Christ any more than Hebrews 2 proves that Psalm 8 speaks exclusively of Christ. In fact scholars today are for the most part convinced that Daniel's son of man is as collective as the four beasts which precede him, and is equivalent to the saints of the Most High. Montgomery speaks for the rest when he says, "The 'accurate' interpretation given later on tells us in so many words what is symbolized by the vision. According to v.18 it is 'the saints of the Most High' who 'shall receive the kingdom'; and in v.27 'sovereignty and dominion ... are given to the people of the saints of the Most High'; i.e., both statements are intentional replicas of v.14."

There are however aspects of this passage which do not agree with the prevailing point of view. First there is the strangeness of the expression "one like a son of man". This figure which Daniel saw in vision was not simply a son of man as in Psalm 8; he was One who had the appearance of a man but could not be identified as belonging to the human race. He was not a child of Adam like the rest of us. He was only like a man, in much the same way as the cherubim of Ezekiel 1:5, the glorified Lord in

Ezekiel 1:26, and the angelic beings in Daniel 8:15 and 10:16, all had the likeness or appearance of human beings. This peculiar expression, One like a son of man, occurs again only in Revelation 1:13 and 14:14 where Christ, and only Christ, is portrayed.

Secondly, the clouds are so frequently the accompaniment of Deity that their presence here must indicate that the Son of Man is a Divine being in his own right. As Leupold says, "They are His carpet, His mark of identification." The glory of the Lord in the tabernacle and temple was constantly manifested by means of a cloud. To mention a few significant passages: Exodus 16:10, "the glory of the Lord appeared in the cloud"; Exodus 19:9, "Behold, I am coming to you in a thick cloud"; Exodus 34:5, "The Lord descended in the cloud"; Leviticus 16:2, "I will appear in the cloud over the mercy seat"; Numbers 11:25, "Then the Lord came down in the cloud"; Psalm 104:3, "He makes the clouds his chariots"; Isaiah 19:1, "Behold, the Lord is riding on a swift cloud"; Nahum 1:3, "the clouds are the dust of his feet."; Matthew 26:64, "from now on you will see the Son of Man seated at the right hand of Power and coming on the clouds of heaven.".

Young observes that among the Jews the Messiah came to be known as *Anani*, Cloudy One, or *Bar-nirli*, Son of a Cloud. Even Montgomery says, "It must be admitted that the earliest interpretation of 'the Son of Man' is Messianic. The term is frequent in the Parables of Enoch, Enoch 37-41, where it occurs 14 times." This remained the most popular interpretation until the mid-nineteenth century when, with the rise of modern criticism, nothing was sacrosanct any more.

Thirdly, it is worth pointing out that the four beasts of Daniel 7 are personal as well as collective, kings as well as kingdoms (vs.17,23). This being the case, there can be no objection to the final kingdom being both personal and collective at the same time. Personally it is represented by the One like a son of man, while collectively it belongs to the people of the saints of the Most High. It is only by virtue of their association with the Son of Man that the saints have any part in this kingdom. But in association with Him, "the greatness of the kingdoms under the whole heaven shall be given to the people of the saints of the Most High" (7:27).

Daniel is greatly alarmed

The effect of the vision on Daniel was similar to the effect the writing on the wall had on Belshazzar. Of both it is said that their colour changed and that their thoughts alarmed them (7:15,28; 5:6). However, it is not said of Daniel, as it is of Belshazzar, that his limbs gave way and his knees knocked together. Belshazzar was obviously terrified by this spectre of a disembodied hand spelling out doom to himself and his nation. But Daniel's anxiety was not for himself at all; what worried him was the character and scope of the vision itself.

The four kingdoms: which are they?

I have left this to last because no definite answer can be given. Certainly Daniel in the first year of Belshazzar can have had no idea where *his* kingdoms would be located. We ask nevertheless: Is there any indication in Daniel (or elsewhere) as to which countries or climes may be involved?

Daniel's visions are cumulative, with each successive revelation throwing light on the earlier ones. In Daniel 2 only the first kingdom is identified. Then chapter 7 expands on the fourth kingdom, the legs, feet and toes of iron and clay. Especially its final embodiment in the little horn is explained in detail. But there is still no indication where this kingdom will rule. Not until the eleventh chapter do we receive any light on this matter, though there is a passing reference in chapter 8.

In Daniel 8:8 and 11:4 there are references to "the four winds of heaven". They speak of the same event, the fourfold division of the kingdom of Greece "towards the four winds of heaven." In chapter 7 the four winds of heaven were seen beating on the Great Sea, and four monsters emerging from the maelstrom. These represent four kings that shall arise out of the earth. Could they be the same as the four kingdoms which rise to power after the break-up of the kingdom of Greece? Is it possible that Daniel would have made the connection?

Two of these kingdoms are identified in Daniel 11. They are the kingdoms of the North and the South. Beyond that there is no further information released. Viewed in prospect, that is as far as the book of

Daniel takes us. The kingdom of Greece would be split into four, two of these would exercise dominion in the lands to the north and south of Israel, the other two would take over the rest of kingdom of Greece, "towards the four winds of heaven."

There was of course an historical fulfilment concerning which Daniel would have known nothing. The kingdom of Alexander the Great was indeed parcelled out between four of his generals in the years following his death. But Daniel's vision, as we can see in retrospect, was not actually fulfilled in these events. Daniel 7 speaks of a future time, the time of the end, when there will be another conflict, resulting in another distribution of the earth's real estate between four future kings "towards the four winds of heaven."

There are references to the four winds of heaven in Jeremiah 49:36, Zechariah 2:6 and 6:5 and Matthew 24:31, and to the four winds of the earth in Mark 13:27 and Revelation 7:1. They all speak of the four points of the compass. The four kingdoms of Daniel 7 will doubtless reach out as far as possible in every direction. This was only partially true of Alexander's dismembered empire; in the future it will be true to a far greater extent.

Daniel Eight

A King of Bold Countenance

The vision of Daniel 8 is closely linked with that of chapter 7. It was seen by Daniel only two years after the previous one, in the third year of Belshazzar, probably 548 BC. Daniel remarks on the fact that the vision was seen by him "after that which appeared to me at the first." He seems to bring the two together in subject matter as well as time. Chapter 8 however is written in Hebrew. After chapter 1 it is the first chapter to be written in Hebrew, and is the first of several visions, all written in Hebrew, with a special bearing on the Jews and Jerusalem in the time of the end (8:17).

Let us remind ourselves of what has been revealed so far. In Daniel 2 four successive empires were portrayed. The fourth of these, which territorially included all the others, is shattered by the kingdom which God Himself will set up. This kingdom will never be destroyed, nor will it be left to another people. Except for the first (Babylon) and the last (the kingdom of God) these kingdoms are not identified in Daniel 2.

In chapter 7 we are introduced to four more kingdoms portrayed by four hybrid monsters. The fourth of these is clearly the same as the fourth of Daniel 2. The other three are not identified; there are indications however that they appear concurrently rather than in succession. This is evident from the fact that when the fourth beast is destroyed the remaining three are permitted to continue for a while. They stand therefore for three kingdoms whose dominions are distinct from those of the fourth beast, but their whereabouts and the extent of their domains are not revealed in Daniel 7.

The spotlight falls on the dreadful fourth beast which was so much stronger and more terrifying than its companions. This beast had ten horns, among which there came up another horn, a little one. This horn assumes the forbidding appearance, blasphemous speech and cowardly actions which point unmistakably to the Antichrist. When however his time is up his dominion is taken away and he himself is consumed and destroyed. It is now the turn of the people of the saints of the Most High to receive the kingdom and the dominion and the greatness of the kingdoms under the whole heaven.

So far a lot of information has been conveyed, but a detailed interpretation has not been forthcoming. This however is remedied in the rest of the book beginning with Daniel 8.

The ram and the goat

Daniel is transported in spirit to Susa in the province of Elam, the summer capital of the Persian kings. Elam was an area between Babylon and Persia, modern Khuzistan, north of the Persian Gulf (Lucas). According to Ron Cantrell, "The city (Susa) sits on four mounds nestled together and is fenced in one side by the Sha'ur river. The area of the city nearest the river is the acropolis, rising about one hundred feet above the river. The tomb of Daniel sits there to this day."

What Daniel saw was a ram with two horns standing on the bank of the Ulai canal. One of the horns was higher than the other, and it was this horn which came up last. The ram proved irresistible: it charged to the west, north, and south with invincible force. It does not say "eastwards" because to the east of Persia (see below) was desert. In the other three directions lay the Fertile Crescent watered by the Tigris and Euphrates rivers. The ram did as it pleased and became great.

Eventually however it was destroyed by a male goat which came from the west, travelling over vast tracts of land at enormous speed. It was enraged against the ram ("moved with choler", *KJV*, a form of the verb which occurs only here and in 11:11). This goat had a conspicuous horn between its eyes, and with it he struck the ram, broke its two horns, and trampled on it as it lay helpless on the ground. But when the goat became great, his conspicuous horn was suddenly broken and in its place came up four more conspicuous horns toward the four winds of heaven. Daniel Berrigan aptly remarks, "In their reign these dubious eminences 'magnify themselves exceedingly' (Daniel 8:8). It would seem that self-delusion in far excess of the human measure is a congenital illness of imperial entities."

The interpretation

The interpretation serves to identify the second and third kingdoms of Daniel 2 as well as the realities portrayed by the ram and the he-goat. Daniel is told, "As for the ram that you saw with the two horns, these are the kings of Media and Persia. And the goat is the king of Greece. And the great horn between his eyes is the first king. As for the horn that was broken, in place of which four others arose, four kingdoms shall arise from his nation, but not with his power" (8:20-22).

There is no question that this vision links up with the previous ones in chapters 2 and 7. Already in chapter 5 we have learned that the Babylonian kingdom, represented by Belshazzar, was divided and given to the Medes and Persians, the first king being Darius the Mede. This is confirmed in chapter 8 where the two horns of the ram correspond to the Medes and Persians, of which the Medes were initially more prominent than the Persians. The ram kingdom of Medo-Persia is now destroyed by the goat kingdom of Greece. Hence the third kingdom of Daniel 2 is shown to be Greece. But the Greek kingdom is short lived so far as its first king is concerned. In his place there arise four more kings towards the four winds of heaven. These are not identified in Daniel 8, but Daniel 11 has a lot to say about two of them, and it is possible that they correspond to the four monsters of Daniel 7. From one of these, in Daniel's vision, there came a little horn which grew exceedingly great towards the south, the east, and the glorious land.

In chapter 2 the four kingdoms were presented to Nebuchadnezzar in the form of all that is most prized among men, gold, silver, brass and iron. In chapters 7 and 8, however, they are shown to Daniel in their true guise as menacing beasts of prey.

Jerusalem holds the key

All these kingdoms had long histories before they assume prophetic significance. What was it that suddenly endowed them with such importance? The answer may be found in their possession of Jerusalem.

Nebuchadnezzar's father, founder of the Neo-Babylonian Empire, was a great conqueror, but he never captured Jerusalem and the Bible consequently is silent concerning him. It was his son, Nebuchadnezzar, who took possession of Jerusalem in 605 BC, and Babylon thereafter immediately assumes a prominent place in Biblical history and prophecy. Likewise Medo-Persia and Greece took control of Jerusalem when they conquered their imperial predecessors. And in the future, it is when the Antichrist makes a seven year pact with the Jews in Jerusalem that his career will hit the headlines in the prophetic scriptures.

Second only to Jerusalem is the importance of Babylon. Babylon was Nebuchadnezzar's magnificent capital. It was a subsidiary capital of the Persian Empire, and the intended capital of Alexander the Great. In the book of Revelation it is "Babylon the Great, mother of prostitutes and of earth's abominations" (17:5). The Antichrist, however, will not make Babylon his capital; quite the contrary he will "devour her flesh and burn her up with fire" (Revelation 17:16). Initially he will be controlled by the woman Babylon who will sit on his heads, but when he is strong enough he will throw her off and reduce her to total desolation (Revelation 18). There is nevertheless truth in the maxim that the Bible is a tale of two cities, Jerusalem and Babylon.

The little horn

The Hebrew for little horn in 8:9 is virtually the same as its Aramaic equivalent in 7:8. That for us is a sure sign that the two represent one and the same person. Liberal scholars have no problem in identifying these two horns which, on their reckoning, correspond to Antiochus Epiphanes in whose days, according to them, Daniel's prophecies were fulfilled and Daniel itself was written. But conservative scholars, be they amillennial or premillennial, have a problem on their hands. Having convinced themselves that the fourth kingdom of Daniel 2 and 7 is Rome, they find themselves unable to identify a little horn which springs from Rome with a little horn which appears on the scene at the latter end of the fragmented kingdom of Greece (8:23). Their solution is to identify the little horn of Daniel 7 with the Antichrist, but the little horn of Daniel 8 with Antiochus Epiphanes. Likewise in Daniel 11, the contemptible person of verses 21-35 they identify with Antiochus Epiphanes, but the king of verse 36 and following they equate with the Antichrist, though there is nothing in the text to support this quantum leap in time and place.

All this muddle would have been avoided if a correct methodology had been followed. Our first concern is to find out what Daniel himself would have expected to happen, and history does not help us here. History is simply a distraction which takes our mind off the real issue. One thing is sure: neither Rome nor Antiochus Epiphanes is mentioned or presupposed anywhere in Daniel. It is unlikely therefore that either of them has any place in the true interpretation of the book.

Similarities between the two little horns are noted by Lucas: "Both became great from small beginnings; both are characterized by blasphemous arrogance; both persecute and prevail against the 'holy ones' for a set period; both ultimately oppose God and are destroyed by God." It is true there is divergence in detail, but as Lucas says, "The differences are not contradictions, but are complementary views resulting from differences in focus in the two visions."

The focus in Daniel 7 is that of the Antichrist on the world stage in the political arena as suits the Aramaic language. In chapter 8 the focus is far more on his outrageous activity against the Jews and their Temple worship, as befits the Hebrew language. According to S.R. Driver, "the impious character and doings [of the little horn] (8:10-12,25) are in all essentials identical with those attributed to the little horn of ch.7 (7:8 end , 20,21,25): as Delitzsch remarks, it is extremely difficult to think that where the description is so similar, two extremely different persons, living in widely different periods of world history, should be intended."

The little horn of Daniel 7 is destroyed and the dominion given to the saints of the Most High (vs.26,27). He belongs therefore to the time of the end and is succeeded by the kingdom of Messiah. Likewise the little horn of Daniel 8 appears "at the latter end of the indignation", at "the appointed time of the end" (v.19), and is broken, but by no human hand (v.25). In chapter 7 he makes war with the saints, wears them down, and prevails over them (vs.21,25); likewise in chapter 8 he destroys mighty men and the people who are the saints (v.24). In chapter 7 he has eyes like the eyes of a man and a mouth speaking great things (v.8); in chapter

8 he is a king of bold countenance who understands riddles (v.23). In chapter 7 he thinks to change times and law (v.25); in chapter 8 he throws truth to the ground, takes away the regular burnt offering and overthrows the place of the sanctuary (vs.11,12). In chapter 7 he speaks words against the Most High (v.25); in chapter 8 he rises up against the Prince of princes (v.25).

One way and another Tregelles' verdict is justified. "The non-identity of the two would involve difficulties of the greatest magnitude - so great that the supposition may be regarded as a moral impossibility." Nor is there any problem or objection to this once it is appreciated that the fourth kingdom of Daniel 2 and 7 is not Rome but one of the divisions of Greece's divided empire.

It will become exceedingly great

The little horn will become exceedingly great towards the south, the east, and the glorious land (8:9). The hub of his kingdom will be modern Syria/ Iraq, the heart of the old Seleucid kingdom of the North (see chap.11). From there he will extend his influence by conquest and diplomacy to the east (Iran and India), to the south (Egypt and Africa), and to the pleasant (glorious, delightful) land of Israel. It says simply "the beauty" or "glory" but there is no doubt that Israel is meant from the following passages.

Daniel 11:16: "And he shall stand in the glorious land."
11:41: "He shall come into the glorious land."
11:45: "he shall pitch his palatial tents between the sea and the glorious holy mountain (the mount of beauty of holiness)."

Jeremiah 3:19: "... and give you a pleasant land, a heritage most beautiful of all nations."

Ezekiel 20:6: "the most glorious of all lands."

The word also means "gazelle", an animal famed for its swiftness of foot, grace and comeliness. In terms of majestic size and splendour Israel was far outstripped by ancient Babylon and Egypt. The Jordan was an insignificant river compared with Abana and Pharpar, the rivers of

Damascus (2 Kings 5:12), let alone the Tigris and Euphrates, rivers of Babylon, and the arterial Nile of Egypt. "The beauty of Jerusalem is God's presence within her" (Ron Cantrill).

Similar epithets for the holy land include "lovely land" (Jeremiah 3:19; Zechariah 7:14; Psalm 106:24); "delightful land" (Mal. 3:12); "beautiful in elevation, the joy of the whole earth" (Psalm 48:2); "the perfection of beauty" (Psalm 50:2). Beauty is in the eye of the beholder. To the faithful Jew Israel is the most beautiful land in the world, and one day soon its beauty will be restored to a degree never seen before except in the inspired dreams of prophets and visionaries (Isaiah 65:17-25; Ezekiel 47:1-12 etc.).

Even to the host of heaven

"It grew great, even to the host of heaven. And some of the host and some of the stars it threw down to the ground and trampled on them" (8:10). The word most frequently used of this 'horn' is *gadol / higdil*, to be or become great. R.H. Charles remarks, "There is a nuance of arrogance and insolence to the word: cf. Psalm 55:12, Jeremiah 48:26." It has already been said of the ram that it became great, and of the goat that it became exceedingly great. The same word is used of the little horn in 8:9,10,11,25 and 11:36,37. Here (8:10) he grows great even to the host of heaven. But what is meant by this? How can a mere man cast down the stars to the ground and trample on them?

Most commentators understand the host of heaven to be a reference to the people of God, on the basis of those passages where Israel is compared to the stars in terms of number or brightness (Daniel 12:3; Genesis 15:5; 22:17). But a different interpretation commends itself. The Antichrist has his counterpart in heaven, the great red dragon with seven heads and ten horns (Revelation 12:3; 13:1). The war on earth is simply the overspill of the war in heaven between Michael and his angels and the devil and his angels. The outcome of the war in heaven is that the dragon is thrown down to the earth, and his angels are thrown down with him (Revelation 12:9). It is possibly this situation which is alluded to in Daniel 8:10.

Goldingay comments, "heaven and earth are not two disconnected worlds. Each underlies the other. Heaven cannot but be involved with earth, earth with heaven." This will be true in the future far more literally than it was in the days of Antiochus Epiphanes where Goldingay finds the fulfilment.

Even as great as the Prince of the host

"He became great, even as great as the Prince of the host" (11). But who is this prince of the host? Most would agree that He is the Lord, especially in view of the following clause, "and the place of his sanctuary was overthrown." The only host mentioned so far has been "the host of heaven" (10). Surely the Prince of the (heavenly) host cannot be anyone less.

The only feasible alternative is Michael, called "one of the chief princes" in Daniel 10:13, "your prince" (10:21), "the great prince" (12:1). He it is who fights against the dragon accompanied by his angels in Revelation 12:7. But Michael is not elsewhere called "prince of the host". The Prince of the host is doubtless the same as the Prince of princes in verse 25.

The Continual (Temple Worship) is taken away

"And the regular burnt offering (*ha-tamid*) was taken away from him (the Lord), and the place of his sanctuary was overthrown" (11). The Continual cannot be limited to the morning and evening sacrifice as in Rabbinic literature. It includes everything to which the word "regular" is attached: the shewbread (Exodus 25:30), the lamp (27:20), the breastplate (28:29), the mitre (28:38), the morning and evening offerings (29:38), the meat and drink offerings (29:41,42), the fire on the altar (Leviticus 6:13), the grain offering (6:20) - in fact the entire Temple worship which this "vainglorious lout" (Berrigan) will bring to an end. The Continual is mentioned also in 11:31 and 12:11 (see also 9:27).

Having made the point that this description speaks of the Antichrist, there is no harm in admitting that Antiochus Epiphanes does serve as a type, understudy, forerunner, of the villain yet to come. This fact is made very obvious in chapter 11, where a future succession of kings culminating in the Antichrist is foreshadowed in the Seleucid kings of the North culminating in Antiochus Epiphanes. This however does not belong to the interpretation of Daniel since Daniel himself, whose understanding of future events it is our aim to discover, would have known nothing of Antiochus Epiphanes. But he would have known a lot about the Antichrist from the revelations granted him in Daniel 7 and 8. Our concern is prophecy not apocrypha. Nevertheless, Antiochus' sweeping prohibition of the laws and customs of the Jews on pain of death, including the temple worship in its entirety as well as circumcision, is a frightening prospect of things to come. These are recorded for our learning in 1 Maccabees.

> And the king sent letters by messengers to Jerusalem and the towns of Judah; he directed them to follow customs strange to the land, to forbid burnt offerings and sacrifices and drink-offerings in the sanctuary, to profane sabbaths and festivals, to defile the sanctuary and the priests, to build altars and sacred precincts and shrines for idols, to sacrifice swine and other unclean animals, and to leave their sons uncircumcised. They were to make themselves abominable by everything unclean and profane, so that they would forget the law and change all the ordinances. He added, 'And whoever does not obey the command of the king shall die. (1 Maccabees 1:44-50 *NRSV*)

> Now on the fifteenth day of Chislev, in the one hundred and forty fifth year (167 BC), they erected a desolating sacrilege on the altar of burnt offering. They also built altars in the surrounding towns of Judah, and offered incense at the doors of the houses and in the streets. The books of the law that they found they tore to pieces and burned with fire. Anyone found possessing the book of the covenant, or anyone who adhered to the law, was condemned to death by decree of the king. They kept using violence against Israel, against those who were found month after month in the towns. On the twenty-fifth day of the month they offered sacrifice on the altar that was on top of the altar of burnt-offering. In accordance with the decree, they put to death the women who had their children circumcised, and their families and those who

circumcised them; and they hung the infants from their mothers' necks. (1 Maccabees 1:54-61)

There can be no doubt that Antiochus Epiphanes was a type and forerunner of the Antichrist yet to come. But so also was Rome and its emperors. In the first century AD the Roman emperors culminating in Nero would have been viewed by Christian believers as fulfilling Daniel 11. For them the Roman Empire was the empire of the last times predicted by Daniel. Rome however did not really fulfil the terms of Daniel's prophecies any more than the kingdom of the Seleucids in the second century BC. The book of Daniel spoke powerfully to the faithful suffering persecution under Antiochus Epiphanes; it spoke just as powerfully to the faithful suffering persecution under Caligula and Nero. But from our perspective it is clear that Daniel was not fulfilled on either of these occasions. That fulfilment still lies in the future, and when it happens there will be no doubt in the minds of believers that what they are seeing and experiencing is indeed the true fulfilment of both Daniel and Revelation.

The transgression that makes desolate

"And a host will be given over to it together with the regular burnt offering because of transgression" (v.12). Many different translations of this difficult sentence have been offered as a glance at the versions will confirm. Apart from the fact that it makes no sense, the chief objection to the above rendering (that of the *ESV*) and others like it is that "host", a masculine noun, is construed with a feminine verb. By means of a minor change of pointing and word division, sense can be restored. If *utseva'oth nathan* is read in place of *utseva' tinnathen*, the following translation is revealed: "And hosts (military contingents) he set against the Continual (temple worship) in transgression, and it (the little horn) cast down (*wat-tashlek*) truth to the ground, and it practised and prospered."

Most of the verbs in verses 9-12 are feminine in agreement with the feminine noun "horn", but the disguise is dropped in verse 11 in the case of *higdil*, "he became great." It is the same in this verse: "and hosts he set ..." Daniel is describing what he saw in vision, hence nearly all the verbs are in the past tense. What is required here is another past tense "he set", not a future imperfect tense as currently pointed in the Hebrew text.

The same act of transgression is referred to in verse 13 where the question is asked, "For how long is the vision concerning the regular burnt offering, the transgression that makes desolate, and the giving over of the sanctuary and host to be trampled underfoot?" The transgression that makes desolate, otherwise called "the abomination that makes desolate" (9:27; 11:31; 12:11), or "the crime causing horror" (Brown-Driver-Briggs), speaks of the desecration of the Temple by means of an idol or image of a blasphemous nature. Our Lord referred to "the abomination of desolation, spoken of by Daniel the prophet" in Matthew 24:15 (Mark 13:14) as an event still future. It cannot therefore have been fulfilled by Antiochus Epiphanes in the second century BC.

In Mark 13:14 "abomination" is construed with a *masculine* participle "standing". The blasphemous act referred to is not simply some "desolating sacrilege" or idol such as Antiochus erected on the altar of burnt offering (1 Maccabees 1:54), but that mentioned in 2 Thessalonians 2:4 where the man of lawlessness "takes his seat in the temple of God, proclaiming himself to be God." This is the transgression that makes desolate which Daniel foresaw, and it has not yet occurred. Clearly there have been delays in the fulfilment of Daniel's prophecies which Daniel himself could not have foreseen.

It will throw truth to the ground

"It cast down truth to the ground, and it acted and prospered" (12). The truth referred to is in context the Law of Moses and the Bible generally. Again in verse 24, "he will prosper and act"; verse 25 "he will cause deceit to prosper"; and 11:36 "he shall prosper till the indignation is accomplished." His success will be phenomenal - but only for the time decreed.

For how long?

That is the all-important question which even angels wish to look into. That question is here answered. From the time the regular worship is abolished, the transgression that makes desolate perpetrated, from the time the sanctuary and host (the Jewish people) are given over to be trodden down -- from that time it will be 2,300 evening-mornings (v.14).

It is generally recognised that 2,300 evening-mornings means 2,300 complete days - evenings and mornings as in Genesis one. Rather similar is the expression "night-day" in 2 Corinthians 11:25, meaning a night and a day. We are to reckon, therefore, 2,300 days from the time the regular worship is abolished and the sanctuary defiled. As we shall shortly discover, this takes place in the middle of the last week of years (9:27). So we are thinking of an extension beyond the end of the week of 1,040 days (2300-1260). Two shorter extensions are detailed in Daniel 12:11,12, one of 30 days and the other of 75 days. It will take even longer, it seems, before the sanctuary is finally put to rights / justified; that is, restored to its rightful state (*ESV*).

But some have thought that only 1,150 complete days are meant, that is 1,150 evenings and 1,150 mornings. This is rejected by Keil "because evening and morning at the creation constituted not the half but the whole day." Pusey says, "The shift of halving the days is one of those monsters, which have disgraced 'scientific exposition' of Hebrew... Standing as the words do before the numeral, the numeral must, according to the principles of all language, apply to the whole. Conceive anyone rendering '*noctes diesque triginta*', '15 days and 15 nights'." According to Pember the meaning is "2300 repetitions of the evening and morning sacrifices - which proves that actual days of 24 hours are intended."

Not fulfilled by Antiochus Epiphanes

Whether taken as 2,300 full days or half that amount, 1,150 days, there is nothing in the history of Antiochus Epiphanes which answers to these numbers. "Reckon as you will", says Leupold, "there is no clear-cut period of either the one or the other length. Then the juggling of facts and figures begins." Undeterred, he goes on to say, "But the very fact that neither the longer period of almost seven years nor the shorter of almost three-and-a-half can be made to tally with known historical facts should serve to cause interpreters to cease continuing along this line."

Lucas agrees: "Attempts to find an exact chronological and historical significance for the number 2,300 have failed to provide any convincing solution." Like Leupold, he resorts to the notion that 2,300 is symbolic for a short significant period. But how such a precise number can be symbolic is not satisfactorily explained. According to Leupold, 2,300 days is six years and 110 days: in other words, not a complete period of seven years. "As it now stands, this number signifies not even a full period of divine judgment." In this he is simply following Keil, but a more obscure way of expressing the idea of an incomplete judgment is difficult to imagine!

Those who interpret this chapter of Antiochus Epiphanes ("near unanimity among commentators", according to Lucas) should have paid more attention to the repeated affirmations that it speaks of the time of the end:

8:17: "the vision is for the time of the end"
8:19: "I will make known to you what shall be at the latter end of the indignation, for it refers to the appointed time of the end"
8:23: "at the latter end of their kingdom, when the transgressors have reached their limit"
8:26: "seal up the vision, for it refers to many days from now."

Leupold correctly observes, "This is an important fact concerning the entire interpretation, and a fact that no man could have discovered by himself. It marks a general approach to the contents of the whole chapter that should be uppermost in the mind of those who busy themselves with this chapter." For Leupold however it does not speak of the end at all, but "serves as a type of what shall transpire at the time of the end of the present world order ... King Antiochus is seen to be a kind of Old Testament antichrist like unto the great Antichrist."

Leon Wood wrestles with the same problem. "In what sense," he asks, "can the period of oppression by Antiochus be called an 'appointed time of the end' and 'the latter portion of the indignation'?" Like Leupold, he finds the solution in Antiochus' typical role as foreshadowing the Antichrist. Far better, surely, to take these statements at their face value. There are many historical characters who serve as types of the Antichrist,

Antiochus being one of them, but this chapter speaks of the time of the end and therefore of the Antichrist himself, not just another type of that evil person.

A king of bold countenance, one who understands riddles (23)

The expression "of bold countenance" is derived from Deuteronomy 28:49-50: "The Lord will bring a nation against you ... a hard-faced nation who shall not respect the old or show mercy to the young." The meaning is hard, unyielding and cruel. A similar expression is applied to the brazen adulteress of Proverbs 7:13. The word "riddle" is used of Samson's riddle to the Philistines (Judges 14), of the hard questions with which the Queen of Sheba tested Solomon (1 Kings 10:1), of the words of the wise (Proverbs 1:6), and of Ezekiel's riddle of the Two Eagles and the Vine (Ezekiel 17). The Antichrist will be "a master of dissimulation, able to conceal his meaning under ambiguous words, and so disguising his real purposes" (S.R. Driver); "a master of Machiavellian arts, master diplomatist, able to deceive 'the very elect'" (Montgomery).

In the words of G.H. Pember (quoted by Lang), "He too will present himself as one in whom are hidden treasures of wisdom and knowledge; and drawing from the vast, though limited, stores of his god - that is, Satan - will dazzle and bewitch men by his solution of the enigmas of life."

His power shall be great

"His power shall be great - but not by his own power; and he shall cause fearful destruction and shall succeed in what he does, and destroy mighty men and the people who are the saints" (24). His power, his throne and great authority are all derived from the dragon (Revelation 13:2). Were he not energized by Satan he would in all truth have no power of his own. In the devil's power he will destroy fearfully: he will overcome the most formidable of foes and especially "the people of the saints". They it is who shortly after will be given "the greatness of the kingdoms under the whole heaven" (7:27).

Without warning he shall destroy many (25)

The same expression "without warning" comes up again in 11:21 and 24. In 11:21 we are told that "He shall come in without warning and obtain the kingdom by flatteries"; and in 11:24 that "without warning he shall come into the richest parts of the province, and he shall do what neither his fathers nor his father's fathers have done, scattering among them plunder, spoils and goods." Lucas remarks that "elsewhere the word always refers to a state of physical contentment or security, and this would apply most readily to the state of the king's victims prior to attack."

The words of Gog come to mind, "I will go up against the land of unwalled villages. I will fall upon the quiet people who dwell securely, all of them dwelling without walls, and having no bars or gates, to seize spoil and carry off plunder ..." (Ezekiel 38:11-12). The Jews will be taken by surprise, having been lulled into a false sense of security by Gog's lavish presents and deceitful promises, confirmed (so they think) by the strong covenant he will make with many for (ostensibly) one week of years (Daniel 9:27).

He shall be broken - but by no human hand (25)

When however he rises up against the Prince of princes, he will be broken without hand. "Not a human or natural agency, but the direct visitation of God will destroy the tyrant" (Montgomery). As we read in 11:45, "he shall pitch his palatial tents between the sea and the glorious holy mountain. Yet he shall come to his end, with none to help him." He will meet his end on the mountains of Israel as all the prophets bear witness (Ezekiel 38:21-23; 39:1-4; Zechariah 12 and 14; Isaiah 30:29-33 etc.). This is the lawless one, "whom the Lord Jesus will kill with the breath of his mouth and bring to nothing by the appearance of his coming" (2 Thessalonians 2:18).

Seal up the vision

Daniel is told to seal up (*sethom*) the vision because it would not be for many days (26). In 12:4 he is given the same instructions: "shut up *(sethom)* the words, and seal *(hethom)* the book until the time of the end." The book was to be shut up and sealed, in the view of most commentators, in order to keep it safe until the time of fulfilment had arrived. That was certainly one reason for putting it away: to keep it safe. But in the view of Goldingay, the verb *satham* more naturally suggests keeping it secret, rather than simply keeping it safe. This is the meaning suggested by Ezekiel 28:3, "You are indeed wiser than Daniel; no secret *(sathum)* is hidden from you." And this meaning is clearly required in Isaiah 29:11: "And the vision of all this has become to you like the words of a book that is sealed *(ha-sepher he-hathum,* cp. Daniel12:4). When men give it to one who can read, saying 'Read this', he says, 'I cannot, for it is sealed!'"

The verb *satham* is used elsewhere of stopping up wells so that the water could no longer flow. In this sense also Daniel was a closed book, its meaning withheld until further notice. Even now we see only dimly as in a burnished mirror (1 Corinthians 13:12). But when the vision starts to be fulfilled, it will shine with a new light. It will then be truly unsealed, a source of knowledge and inspiration to all who read it.

Interestingly, the apostle John is given the opposite instruction. He is told not to seal the words of the prophecy, for the time is near (Revelation 22:10). In the first century AD the time of fulfilment had arrived. This was true of Daniel as well as Revelation. But due to continued unbelief and hardness of heart, its fulfilment was again postponed for an undisclosed period of time at the end of the Acts. It then became a book as closed and sealed as ever Daniel was.

Daniel is horrified

Daniel was so appalled at the revelation he had received that he was physically unwell for several days. The awful punishment that his people would receive at the hands of the little horn was almost more than he could bear. He did not fully understand the vision, but he understood enough to be horrified at the prospect.

Daniel Nine

Seventy Years and Seventy Weeks of Years

It was the first year of Darius the Mede, 538 BC, one year after the fall of Babylon and the death of Belshazzar. Daniel's thoughts turn to Jeremiah's predictions concerning the length the Jews would remain captive in Babylon, predictions which could never have been far from his thoughts. Jeremiah had predicted that the Lord would punish "the king of Babylon and that nation" when the seventy years were accomplished for Babylon (Jeremiah 25:12). He had also predicted that when the seventy years were completed, the Lord would visit them, fulfil His promise and bring them back to this place, namely Judah and Jerusalem (29:10). Putting two and two together he could only have concluded that the time of restoration had arrived. Babylon had already fallen (on 12 October 539), but there were still two years to run before the termination of the seventy-year period, 605-536.

Daniel knew however that restoration was not an automatic eventuality which would happen of necessity at the end of the seventy years. Like all God's blessings it was dependent on a right frame of mind, on sincere repentance, on deep regret for past rebellion and unbelief, and a set resolve to seek and serve the Lord. Had not Jeremiah himself said as much? "Then you will call upon me and come and pray to me, and I will hear you. You will seek me and find me. When you seek me with all your heart, I will be found by you, declares the Lord, and I will restore your fortunes and gather you from all the nations ..." (Jeremiah 29:12-14).

Since this was the precondition, Daniel resolved to carry it out to the letter, including fasting in sackcloth and ashes. In total contrition he repented on behalf of his people, confessing their sins and beseeching the Lord for forgiveness and restoration.

Daniel's prayer

Daniel's prayer of humble confession revolves around two subjects, the city and the people. In verses 3-15 he confesses the sin of the nation, including himself among the guilty people whose rebellion had been the cause of their present shame and calamity. Repeatedly he uses the first person plural: we have sinned, we have not listened, etc. There were certainly others who shared his concern, but sadly Daniel prayed on his own. The people in general, those on whose behalf Daniel prayed, were too preoccupied pursuing their daily business to be exercised about matters of such profound spiritual importance as the restoration of Jerusalem and their return from exile.

In the concluding part of his prayer, verses 16-19, Daniel offers up his specific requests for the city and people, not forgetting the sanctuary in ruins. "O Lord, according to all your righteous acts, let your anger and your wrath turn away from your city Jerusalem, your holy city" (v.16); "O Lord, make your face to shine upon your sanctuary, which is desolate" (v.17); "Open your eyes and see our desolations, and the city that is called by your name" (v.18); "Delay not, for your own sake, O my God, because your city and your people are called by your name" (v.19).

Gabriel is sent with the answer

It was while Daniel was still confessing the sin of his people and making request for God's holy hill Jerusalem, that Gabriel was sent with the answer to his prayer. He came in swift flight at the time of the evening sacrifice with the express purpose of giving Daniel insight and understanding. He begins, "Seventy weeks is decreed concerning your people and your holy city" (v.24). These were the two main concerns of Daniel's prayer, and they are the two subjects of Gabriel's revelation.

"Seventy weeks is decreed." "The singular verb after the plural subject is to be explained on the ground that the seventy weeks are regarded as a unit of time" (R.H. Charles). Keil agrees: "The seventy sevens are to be viewed as a whole, as a continued period of seventy seven times following each other." As initially revealed, as seen in prospect, the seventy weeks were expected to run their course without a break, as an integral unit of time. If in fact, as it subsequently transpired, there was a break, or breaks, in the succession of weeks, this was due to events long after the time of Daniel. Certainly there is nothing in the prophecy itself to suggest a break of any kind, and this is a point of great importance for the understanding of Daniel as a whole.

The word translated "week" means a period divisible by seven, a heptad or hebdomad. In the sense of ordinary weeks of seven days the word is usually feminine plural, but the masculine plural (as here) is found also in Daniel 10:2,3 (lit. "three weeks, days", that is, three full weeks). In the present context day-weeks would be inappropriate. Seventy day-weeks would be only sixteen months which would reduce the prophecy to absurdity. We are thinking therefore of seventy year -weeks, or 490 years.

The present revelation is related to Jeremiah's prophecy of seventy years, not simply seventy years but now seventy weeks of years: this is the length of time they would now have to wait before they could expect complete restoration. This involved a radical revision of Jeremiah's time schedule. If the whole nation had repented in the way Daniel did, they might have experienced complete restoration without delay. But now they would have to wait a long long time, 490 years, before their national destiny could be realised.

Pember points out that "The Seventy Sevens are separated off, not only upon the people, but also upon the City - that is, upon the people in connection with the City. Therefore, during the whole course of the sevens the Jews must be dwelling in their own country."

Six lasting benefits

The termination of the Seventy Weeks would bring in six lasting benefits to Israel according to verse 24. These divide into two groups of three, the first group dealing with the forgiveness and removal of sin, and the second group with the fulfilment of Israel's national hopes.

(1) "To shut up" or "put an end to" the transgression. The Hebrew gives us a choice: either to shut up / restrain (the *Kethiv*, or written text) or to finish / put an end to (the *Qere*, or text to be read

according to the Massoretic editors). Keil regards the *Kethiv* as preferable in most cases. Probably we should read *li-klo'* in the sense of restrain, shut up, hold in prison. Hence *kele'*, a prison.

Either way, the termination of "the transgression" is indicated. But what is meant by this term? Three words are used for Israel's sin in this verse, transgression, sins and iniquity. Between them they comprehensively sum up every aspect of Israel's rebellion against God, as for example in Exodus 34:6,7 where all three are found: "The Lord, the Lord, a God merciful and gracious ... forgiving iniquity and transgression and sin..." The basic meaning of "transgression" (*pesha'*) is rebellion. The definite article depicts Israel's repeated rebellion against God as one huge act of rebellion or mutiny which is now forgiven and forgotten. There may also be an allusion to the transgression that makes desolate in Daniel 8:13. That also would be shut up or put away.

(2) "To seal up" or "put an end to" sins. Once again the Hebrew gives us a choice of verbs. The *Qere*, put an end to, may be imported from 8:23 "when the transgressors have reached their limit (come to a full end)". To seal up sins follows on naturally from their restraint and imprisonment, in the same way as the lions' den was sealed after Daniel had been imprisoned there.

Daniel had prayed, "let your anger and your wrath turn away from your city Jerusalem, your holy city, because for our sins, and for the iniquities of our fathers, Jerusalem and your people have become a byword among all who are around us" (v.16). Not till Israel's sins, the cause of Jerusalem's shameful condition, were removed could there be any change for the better. This would take place, Daniel is assured, but not before the end of the Seventy Weeks.

(3) "To atone for iniquity". This iniquity is that of the fathers mentioned in verse 16. It was of course by the death of Christ that atonement was made for sin and iniquity (1 John 2:2; 4:10). It is He who "has appeared once for all at the end of the ages to put away sin by the sacrifice of himself" (Hebrews 9:26). The sacrifice was made "once for all", but its application to Israel does not take place until Christ's return in glory. It is part and parcel of the new covenant that the Lord will

forgive their iniquity and remember their sin no more (Jeremiah 31:34). "On that day there shall be a fountain opened for the house of David and the inhabitants of Jerusalem, to cleanse them from sin and uncleanness" (Zechariah 13:1). Only when "the Deliverer will come from Zion" will He "banish ungodliness from Jacob" and "take away their sins" (Romans 11:26-27). According to Isaiah 59:20, quoted here by Paul, "a Redeemer will come to Zion, to those in Jacob who turn from transgression."

(4) "To bring in everlasting righteousness", or "the righteousness of ages". There are not many places where *'olam*, age, occurs in the plural as here. One such passage is Isaiah 26:4, "for the Lord God is an everlasting rock (or "rock of ages")." Another, more relevant for our present purpose, is Isaiah 45:17, "But Israel is saved by the Lord with everlasting salvation (salvation of ages); you shall not be put to shame or confounded to all eternity (to ages of perpetuity)." Yet another which may be compared is Isaiah 60:21, "Your people shall all be righteous; they shall possess the land for ever (to an age)."

(5) "To seal both vision and prophet". The vision was sealed in 8:26 because it referred to a time many days removed. But a different word is there used for "seal", *satham*, to stop up, rather than *hatham*, to seal. Vision and prophet will be sealed up when they have served their purpose, when their forecasts have all been translated into fact. The bulk of prophecy relates to the last days, to the stressful period preceding the (second) coming of Christ and the transformation which follows. There can be no sealing up of vision and prophet so long as these prophecies remain unfulfilled. When sin is sealed up, vision and prophecy shall also be laid aside.

(6) "To anoint a most holy place". The phrase "most holy" (lit. "holy of holies") is here without the definite article. When used with the article it means either the most holy place (e.g. Exodus 26:33-34; 2 Chronicles 3:8; 4:22) or the most holy things (e.g. Numbers 4:4,19). The simple *qodesh qodashim* is normally used adjectivally in the sense of "most holy" with reference to many things relating to the Temple worship (the altar of burnt offering, the altar of incense, the ark of the covenant, offerings, vessels, spices etc.). Even in Ezekiel 45:3 where it occurs in apposition to the (millennial) sanctuary, it has an adjectival flavour: "the

sanctuary most holy" or "the sanctuary, a most holy (place)."

In one passage, 1 Chronicles 23:13, strangely mistranslated in our standard versions, it is used personally of Aaron, "to anoint him (to be) a most holy (person)". Daniel 9:24 is unique in that "most holy" is not used to qualify something or someone else. Keil cannot be far wrong in saying that "the reference is to the anointing of a new sanctuary, temple, or most holy place." It is not the holy place of the second temple which is meant, since that would require the definite article, "but a new holy of holies which should be in the place of the holy of holies of the tabernacle and the temple of Solomon."

The point is frequently made that the Tabernacle was anointed (Exodus 40), but that subsequent temples, those of Solomon and Zerubbabel, were not, since these were considered no more than a continuation of the Tabernacle in the wilderness. There may be a reference to the purification of the sanctuary mentioned in Daniel 8:14, which will take place 1,040 days (2,300 – 1,260 days; that is 33.5 months) after the close of the seventieth week.

Those who choose to see no further than Antiochus Epiphanes can have no idea of the length and breadth of these promises. Nor can those who limit their application to the first coming of Christ and to events of that time. For their fulfilment they all depend, it is true, on His once-for-all sacrifice on the cross, but so far as Israel and Jerusalem, people and city, are concerned, none of them has yet been fulfilled or indeed begun to be fulfilled. We can only agree with Pember that "the close of the Seventy Sevens must coincide with the end of the present order of things and the beginning of the Coming or Millennial Age."

The going out of the word to restore and build Jerusalem (25)

Another word which "went out" is mentioned in verse 23. This was the word of Gabriel, the revealing angel, and its subject-matter the vision of the Seventy Weeks. The word which goes forth to restore and build Jerusalem is a different command altogether, one which will give authorization to restore and build Jerusalem. The words "restore" and "build" refer to two separate acts or events, not simply "build again" as some have translated.

The first verb *le-hashiv*, to bring back or restore, occurs in Jeremiah 29:10 in connection with the prophecy of the seventy years: "I will fulfil to you my promise and bring you back to this place." And the second verb, to build, in Jeremiah 30:18, "the city shall be rebuilt on its mound, and the palace shall stand where it used to be." There is no doubt that Jeremiah expected the return from exile and the rebuilding of Jerusalem to follow immediately the expiry of the seventy-year term.

What would Daniel have expected?

What would Daniel have expected to happen, that is the question? We need to put ourselves in his shoes and to view the situation from his perspective. The year is the first year of Darius the Mede, 538 BC by our reckoning. This was before any of the decrees in Ezra and Nehemiah. Daniel knew nothing of these: all he had to go on were the prophecies of Isaiah and Jeremiah and the words of Gabriel now being uttered. How would he have seen the likely turn of events?

Without a doubt Daniel would have expected Cyrus to issue the command to restore the exiles and to rebuild Jerusalem. For this he had the express word of the Lord to Isaiah. Of Cyrus the Lord had said, "He is my shepherd, and he shall fulfil all my purpose, saying of Jerusalem, 'She shall be built', and of the temple, 'Your foundation shall be laid'" (Isaiah 44:28). And again, "he shall build my city and set my exiles free, not for price or reward, says the Lord of hosts" (Isaiah 45:13). These prophecies, coupled with those of Jeremiah, would have given Daniel solid scriptural ground for expecting the word to go forth at the close of the seventy-year period. The seventy years began in 605 with his own deportation to Babylon in the third year of Jehoiakim. They were due to end therefore in 536.

Daniel must have awaited the year 536 with growing apprehension. He was a wise man who knew the ways of the Lord better than anyone else in his generation (Ezekiel 28:3). Would the Lord answer his prayer, "Delay not, for your own sake, O my God, because your city and your people are called by your name" (v.19)? Or, in view of the indifference of most of his fellow exiles, would He find it impossible to implement His promises so soon?

Cyrus' decree

Daniel lived to see Cyrus' decree, issued in the first year of his reign over the Chaldeans (536). He would have seen both the text and its outcome in the short term. The text is given in three places, 2 Chronicles 36:23, Ezra 1:2-4 and 6:3-5. These are admittedly only a summary, but they are agreed on the most important point: that the house of God in Jerusalem should be rebuilt. No mention is made of the city notwithstanding the clear directives in Isaiah and Jeremiah.

Certainly a start was made on the Temple. The foundation stone was laid amidst a fanfare of trumpets and cymbals and antiphonal singing (Ezra 3:10-11). But sadly the work was not allowed to continue, since "the people of the land discouraged the people of Judah and made them afraid to build and bribed counsellors against them to frustrate their purpose, all the days of Cyrus king of Persia, even until the reign of Darius king of Persia" (4:4-5). As Sir Robert Anderson once said, "a few refractory Samaritans were allowed to thwart the execution of this the most solemn edict ever issued by an Eastern despot, an edict in respect of which a Divine sanction seemed to confirm the unalterable will of a Medo-Persian king." (p.56)

Cyrus' decree came to nothing and had to be reactivated by his successor bar one, Darius I, in 520 BC, as described in Ezra 6. Even then, however, there was no mention of the city. Daniel's prophetic programme was already in difficulties. There was no official word to restore and rebuild the city in either 536 or 520. There is reason to believe that time is only considered in Daniel to the extent that it falls within the 70 years of exile and the 70 weeks of years of Daniel 9. These two periods comprise the head and the body of Nebuchadnezzar's Great Image. If that is correct, the years following 536 are not accounted for in Daniel. Already the body of the image is severed from the head of gold even in Daniel's lifetime, and must now await an official word from a Persian king before it could be resumed.

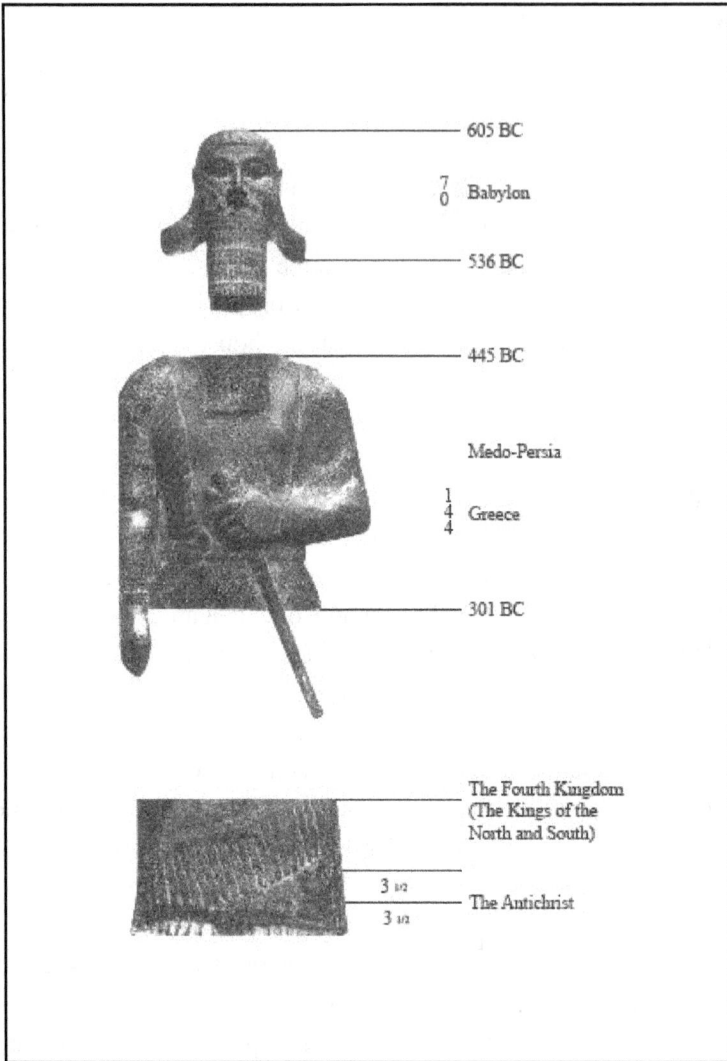

605 BC

7
0 Babylon

536 BC

445 BC

Medo-Persia

1
4 Greece
4

301 BC

The Fourth Kingdom
(The Kings of the
North and South)

3 1/2
The Antichrist
3 1/2

When was that official word?

It was certainly not in 536 or 520, but could it have been in 458 when, in the seventh year of Artaxerxes, Ezra went up to Jerusalem. Ezra went up armed with a letter from King Artaxerxes the text of which is given in Ezra 7:11-26. Ample provision is made by the king "for the house of their God that is in Jerusalem", "to beautify the house of the Lord that is in

Jerusalem" (vs.16,27), but one reads this letter in vain to find any reference to rebuilding the city. Permission to rebuild, or any provision whatsoever for the city, is conspicuously absent.

It is nevertheless true that in the early years of Artaxerxes' reign there was an attempt to rebuild the city. This unauthorized attempt met with stiff resistance from the Jews' adversaries as had their attempt to rebuild the Temple in 536. They sent a letter of complaint "in the days of Artaxerxes" advising the king that the Jews "are rebuilding that rebellious and wicked city. They are finishing the walls and repairing the foundations" (Ezra 4:7-16). Their complaint had the desired effect. The king sent an answer commanding the work to cease immediately. "Therefore make a decree that these men be made to cease, and that this city be not rebuilt, until a decree is made by me. And take care not to be slack in this matter. Why should damage grow to the hurt of the king?" (4:17-22).

Rehum and Shimshai, the Jews' adversaries, were only too happy to oblige: "they went in haste to the Jews at Jerusalem and by force and power made them cease" (4:23). Artaxerxes makes it clear that the city should not be rebuilt until a decree is made by him. What clearer proof could we ask for that no decree to rebuild Jerusalem had been issued prior to Artaxerxes' reign?

It should be explained that Ezra 4:6-23 is chronologically out of place. Here two letters of complaint sent to Cyrus' successors are inserted in the section relating to Cyrus, so bringing together all the attempts by the Jews' adversaries to oppose the work of God. The first letter is an accusation against the Jews in the reign of Xerxes, 486-465 BC (4:9), and the second a letter against Jerusalem sent in the reign of Artaxerxes, 464-423 (4:7-23). This entire section is parenthetical to the chapter as a whole. Hence verse 24 carries on from verse 5 as if nothing intervened.

The edict of Artaxerxes' twentieth year

So the attempt to rebuild Jerusalem in the reign of Artaxerxes was brought to an abrupt end by order of the king. News of this setback reached the ears of Nehemiah in Susa. It was the month Kislev, the ninth month, in the twentieth year of Artaxerxes, 446 BC. The information was conveyed by Hanani, Nehemiah's brother, and others from Judah. They said to him, "The remnant there in the province who had survived the exile is in great trouble and shame. The wall of Jerusalem is broken down, and its gates are destroyed by fire" (Nehemiah 1:3). Naturally Nehemiah was deeply distressed that this attempt to rebuild Jerusalem had ended so ignominiously.

Less than four months later, in Nisan (March-April) of 445, the king noticed how downcast his cupbearer was looking and asked him the reason for his sadness. Fearfully Nehemiah replied, "Let the king live for ever! Why should not my face be sad, when the city, the place of my fathers' graves, lies in ruins, and its gates have been destroyed by fire?" "What are you requesting?" asked the king. Having uttered a silent prayer, Nehemiah replied, "If it pleases the king, and if your servant has found favour in your sight, that you send me to Judah, to the city of my fathers' graves, *that I may rebuild it*." Having inquired how long Nehemiah would be away, the king was pleased to dispatch Nehemiah to Jerusalem with permission to rebuild the city. He gave him letters of safe conduct to pass through the province of his enemies Beyond the River and sufficient timber from the king's forest to build the walls of the city, the fortress of the temple and his own house (Nehemiah 2:1-8).

The facts speak for themselves. Not till the twentieth year of Artaxerxes (445 BC) was the work of rebuilding Jerusalem begun in earnest with the written approval of the king himself. The wall was finished in 52 days on the 25th Elul (the sixth month). But that was only the beginning. "The city was wide and large, but the people within it were few, and no houses had been rebuilt" (Nehemiah 7:4). Shortly after they cast lots to bring one person out of ten to live in Jerusalem, while nine out of ten remained in the provinces. In this way the population of Jerusalem was swelled to rather more than 3,000 (Nehemiah 11). The entire work of rebuilding Jerusalem took all of 49 years if that is the significance of the first seven weeks of Daniel's prophecy.

A possible objection

Should it be objected that there was no decree or formal edict in the twentieth year of Artaxerxes, it should suffice to observe that Daniel 9:25 does not require an official decree. Only "the word" was needed, the word of command, and that is precisely what Nehemiah received. This word was backed up with "letters" to the governors of the province Beyond the River and to Asaph, the keeper of the king's forest. Nehemiah was granted exactly what he asked for, "for the good hand of my God was upon me", he says.

The king's word was all that was needed. Haman's fate was sealed as soon as the word had left the king's mouth (Esther 7:8). The king's word simply confirmed that of the Lord and accomplished the Lord's purpose (Isaiah 55:11).

What say the commentators?

The commentators for the most part are not convinced. Keil and Young both prefer Cyrus' decree. Young objects to Artaxerxes' decree on the grounds:

(1) Of Isaiah 45:1,13; 44:28 where Cyrus is assumed to be the one to rebuild Jerusalem. But Isaiah's forecast was postponed, we believe, owing to the indifference and unbelief of the people.

(2) Ezra pictures Jerusalem as already existing in 4:12 and 9:9. Ezra 4:4 has already been explained. Ezra 9:9 does not refer to a wall as such, but a fence such as was used to surround a vineyard. Keil explains it as "an image of protection from the incursion and attacks of enemies. Such a wall has been given them in Judah and Jerusalem by the kings of Persia." This was not a city wall but "protection in Judea and Jerusalem" (*ESV*).

(3) In Haggai 1:4 the prophet inquires, "Is it time for you yourselves to dwell in your panelled houses while this house (the temple) lies in ruins?" But who said these panelled houses were situated in Jerusalem? Even if they were, it takes more than a few sporadic houses to constitute a city restored and rebuilt.

Leupold has no time whatsoever for Artaxerxes' decree. "To find in this episode, which is mentioned briefly in passing, and which almost eludes us at a casual reading, the important decree for the rebuilding of Jerusalem ... quite taxes our credulity ... To construe this to be the command for the restoration of the city as such disregards the plain meaning of words." But the Bible calls for more than a casual reading. A careful attention to the plain meaning of words fully confirms our interpretation.

In the opinion of Leon Wood none of the three main decrees in Ezra and Nehemiah concerned directly the restoration and rebuilding of Jerusalem. That of 445 BC concerned only "the rebuilding of the walls, when, long before, most of the city had been rebuilt." But that is not the case. When Nehemiah stood before Artaxerxes the city lay in ruins and its gates were destroyed by fire (Nehemiah 1:3). Is that is what is meant by a city restored and rebuilt (Daniel 9:25)?

Ernest Lucas says, "As far as the context of the 'word' is concerned, it seems to point to one of Jeremiah's prophecies (ch. 29 or 30-31) or to Artaxerxes' decree in 445." In common with most critics he favours Jeremiah's prophecies, since the first seven weeks (49 years) can then be referred to the period of exile. Before the exile, however, the word oft repeated was to destroy Jerusalem, not to rebuild it!

Pember complains that "of four decrees which are mentioned in the Scriptures, the majority of commentators have selected those which did not fulfil the conditions of the prophecy, with a perversity which admits of but one explanation." This, he says, is "the pernicious practice of deciding what a prophecy means before it has been studied, and of ignoring any details which will not yield themselves to the fore-determined conclusion" (p.336). One is aware of this pernicious practice, not here alone, but over and over again in commentaries on Daniel.

The reading of many commentators is at best a mixed blessing. One should however always pay heed to people's objections. Valid objections need to be carefully weighed and considered; invalid ones tend to confirm one's own interpretation. The decree of Artaxerxes' 20th year is the only one which fits the bill. This is the only one which relates to the restoring and building of the city. A city fully restored requires more than a few makeshift houses; it requires "squares and moat" (Daniel 9:25) and a city wall. None of these existed before the time of Nehemiah.

The true text

The text followed here is that of the *KJV* and *NIV*. The *ESV* follows the Massoretic punctuation in separating the "seven weeks" from the "sixty-two weeks".

(*NIV*)	(*ESV*)
Know and understand this: From the issuing of the decree to restore and rebuild Jerusalem until the Anointed One, the rule, comes, there will be seven 'sevens' and sixty-two sevens. It will be rebuilt with streets and a trench, but in times of trouble. After sixty-two 'sevens', the Anointed One will be cut off and will have nothing. The people of the ruler who will come will destroy the city and the sanctuary. The end will come like a flood: War will continue until the end, and desolations have been decreed. He will confirm a covenant with many for one 'seven'. In the middle of the 'seven' he will put an end to sacrifice and offering. And on a wing [of the temple] he will set up an abomination that causes desolation, until the end that is decreed is poured out on him.	Know therefore and understand that from the going out of the word to restore and build Jerusalem to the coming of an anointed one, a prince, there shall be seven weeks. Then for sixty-two weeks it shall be built again with squares and moat, but in a troubled time. And after the sixty-two weeks, an anointed one shall be cut off and shall have nothing. And the people of the prince who is to come shall destroy the city and the sanctuary. Its end shall come with a flood, and to the end there shall be war. Desolations are decreed. And he shall make a strong covenant with many for one week, and for half of the week he shall put an end to sacrifice and offering. And on the wing of abominations shall come one who makes desolate, until the decreed end is poured out on the desolator.

The Septuagint (at 27a), Theodotion, Syriac and Vulgate all construe the 7 and 62 as one numeral, and this is followed by the *KJV, NIV, ASV, NASB, Jerusalem*, and many others. The Massoretic punctuation is later than the ancient versions just mentioned, and is suspect for at least two reasons. First, it makes no sense. To say that from the going forth of the word to restore and build Jerusalem to an anointed one, a prince, will be seven weeks is meaningless on any interpretation. Secondly, it has all the hallmarks of an anti-Christian polemic. A prophecy which points so clearly to the death of Christ was an offence to the Jews. Not wanting this to appear in the authorized text, they took measures to conceal it without actually altering the consonantal text or the order of words.

Keil, while accepting the Massoretic punctuation as probably correct, candidly remarks, "it first was adopted by the Massoretes, and only shows the interpretation of these men, without at all furnishing any guarantee for its correctness." This being the case, there is every reason for rejecting it.

The following is a revised translation of verses 24-27 in which certain changes have been made. These changes will be justified and explained in succeeding paragraphs.

> Seventy weeks is decreed upon your people and upon your holy city, to shut up the transgression, and to seal up the vision for iniquity, and to bring in everlasting righteousness, and to seal up vision and prophecy, and to anoint a most holy (place). Know therefore and understand: From the going forth of the word to restore and to build Jerusalem until Messiah, prince, shall be seven weeks and sixty-two weeks. It shall be built again with squares and moat, but in distressful times. And after the sixty-two weeks will Messiah be cut off, not having either the city or the sanctuary. The invading prince will destroy a people and its end will be with a flood, and until the end of the war desolations are determined. And he will make a strong covenant with the many for one week, and for half the week he will cause sacrifice and offerings to cease, and upon a wing (of the temple) will be desolating abominations, even until a final end, the one determined, is poured out on the desolator.

Squares and moat

It shall be built again with squares and moat. According to Montgomery, "By street (*rehov*), properly 'broadway, plaza', are meant the broad spaces, generally inside the city gates, the centre of city life, and by synecdoche standing for the city." As for the word translated moat, this "has now been identified with that sense in the mixed Hebrew-Aramaic Zakar Inscription of the 8th cent. B.C.; the word is also known from the Talmud. As 'street' stands for the interior of the city, so moat for the line of circumvallation, and the two items present a graphic picture of the complete restoration."

It must surely be obvious that no such restoration took place prior to 445 BC.

Anointed One

Mashiah, anointed one or messiah, is not elsewhere used as a proper name unless it is so used in Psalm 2:2, "Why do the nations rage ... against the Lord and against His anointed." Otherwise it is applied to Israel's kings, high priests, patriarchs and prophets (Psalm 105:15), and even Cyrus (Isaiah 45:1, "Thus says the Lord to his anointed, to Cyrus"). When however we turn to the New Testament, "Messiah" is on everyone's lips (e.g. John 1:41 "We have found the Messiah"; John 4:25 "I know that Messiah is coming"). Messiah is here as much a proper name as its Greek equivalent, Christ.

Prince

Various kinds of leaders are called *nagid*, especially the kings of Israel. In Ezekiel 28:2 it is used of the prince of Tyre who was saying, "I am a god (or God), I sit in the seat of the gods, in the heart of the seas." In Daniel 9:26 the same word is used of the "prince who is to come", a man of the same mould as the prince of Tyre. In Daniel 11:22 there is a reference to the "prince of the covenant", a prince or leader of Israel apparently.

Daniel 9 tells the story of two princes, Messiah prince and the coming prince. The coming prince is the Antichrist whose evil character is described in ever more lurid colours in chapters 7,8,9 and 11. Messiah prince is the Prince of princes (*sar sarim*, 8:25), the Son of man to whom "was given dominion and glory and a kingdom, that all peoples, nations and languages should serve him" (7:14).

Messiah shall be cut off

The verb "cut off" (*karath*) is used characteristically of the death penalty. The first occurrence is in Genesis 9:11, "never again shall all flesh be cut off", and thereafter frequently in the books of the Law. Keil says this verb "signifies to be rooted up, destroyed, annihilated, and denotes generally a violent kind of death, though not always, but only the uprooting from among the living, or from the congregation, and is therefore the usual expression for the destruction of the ungodly - e.g. Psalm 37:9, Proverbs 2:22 - without particularly designating the manner in which this is done."

In Isaiah 53:8 a different verb is employed: "He was cut off (*gazar*) out of the land of the living, stricken for the transgression of my people."

And shall have nothing

Literally, "and there is not to him". The sentence appears to be cut short, since it is usual for this expression to be followed by a statement of what the subject is lacking: "and there is not to him such-and-such." There are several ways of dealing with this construction.

(1) The usual translation may stand: "and shall have nothing." There is a similar case in Exodus 22:2(3): "if (the thief) has nothing, then he shall be sold for his theft." The meaning is, if the thief has nothing wherewith to pay ...

(2) The construction may be elliptical. If that is the case, the complete phrase is found in Daniel 11:45, "and there is not a helper to him." So the meaning may be that Messiah will be cut off with no-one to help Him. According to Pember, the subject must be gleaned from the context: "And He shall not have the glory and power which of right

belong to Him as the Messiah." This makes good sense, but one cannot help asking why the most important word (or words) is omitted.

(3) The most satisfactory solution in my view is to take the two words which follow in the Hebrew, "either the city or the sanctuary", and to suppose that they have been wrongly separated from the clause in question. The whole verse may then be translated, "And after 62 weeks Messiah will be cut off, having neither the city nor the sanctuary. The coming prince will destroy the people, and its end (shall be) with a flood. And to the end of the war desolations are determined." This reconstruction clarifies what follows as well as what precedes, and is accepted by both Lucas and Goldingay.

The city and the sanctuary rightfully belong to the Lord. Daniel had prayed, "your city Jerusalem, your holy hill ... make your face to shine upon your sanctuary" (9:16,17,19). But Messiah would be cut off in possession of neither. Not until the decreed end is poured out on the desolator will He regain them. Then Jerusalem will be called "the city of the Lord, the Zion of the Holy One of Israel" (Isaiah 60:14). And even "the pots in the house of the Lord shall be as bowls before the altar. And every pot in Jerusalem and Judah shall be holy to the Lord of hosts!" (Zechariah 14:20-21). What a remarkable repossession!

The coming prince will destroy the people

According to the usual translations, the people of the prince yet to come shall destroy the city and the sanctuary. But there is no evidence that the Antichrist will destroy either the city or the sanctuary. He will be permitted to occupy and trample the holy city and the outer courts of the Temple (Luke 21:24; Revelation 11:1-3), but that is the extent of his mandate. In Zechariah 14:1-2 the city is taken, the houses plundered and the women raped. Half of the city goes into exile, but the rest will not be cut off from the city. The Temple is horribly defiled and misused, but it is not physically destroyed. The very fact that the Antichrist puts a stop to sacrifice and oblation and sets up the abomination of desolation presupposes the continued existence of the Temple itself.

This goes to show that the destruction of Jerusalem by the Romans is not in the picture here. AD 70 falls in the gap between the sixty-ninth and the seventieth weeks. That gap should never have occurred if the succession of weeks had run without a break as Daniel was led to believe. We know in retrospect that there was a gap at this point, but in Daniel it is simply passed over as if having no existence..

But the fate of the people, Jerusalem's population, is another matter altogether. We know from 8:24 that "he will destroy (same verb as in 9:26) mighty men and the people of the saints." Likewise 7:21, "this horn made war with the saints and prevailed over them"; 11:33, "And the wise among the people shall make many understand, though for some days they shall stumble by sword and flame, by captivity and plunder"; 12:7, "when the shattering of the power of the holy people comes to an end ..."

The word translated "coming" is used aggressively of an invader. The same participle, *ha-ba'*, occurs in Daniel 11:16, "But he who comes (namely, the king of the North) against him shall do as he wills"; and the verb itself in sixteen other places in this chapter. "The coming prince" might more suitably be translated "the king, the aggressor (or invader)".

And its end with the flood

It is the people who are destroyed by the flood not the Antichrist himself. He is responsible for it, not destroyed by it (11:22; Revelation 12:15). The same event is referred to in 11:22 where "contemptible person" is another name for the coming prince. A literal translation of 11:22 is as follows: "With the arms of the flood will they be flooded from before him, and they will be broken, as also the prince of the covenant." The word flood is often used of an invading army coming in like a tidal wave (Jeremiah 47:2; Nahum 1:8; Daniel 11:26). Isaiah 8:6-8 describes exactly what is meant:

> Because this people has rejected the gently flowing waters of Shiloah and rejoices over Rezin and the son of Remaliah, therefore the Lord of hosts is about to bring against them the mighty floodwaters of the River - the king of Assyria with all his pomp. It will overflow all its channels, run over all its banks, and sweep on

into Judah, swirling over it, passing through it and reaching up to the neck. Its outspread wings will cover the breadth of your land, O Immanuel! (*NIV*)

A strong covenant (v.27)

"And he shall make a strong covenant with the many for one week." This reference goes back in time; it preceded the invasion described in v.26. This covenant or agreement the Antichrist will make with the majority for a period of seven years. They will be led to understand that after seven years it will be renewed for a further seven years, and so on. They are lulled into a mindset of complacency and material wellbeing, not realising that the Antichrist has no intention of keeping it. The word "many" is sometimes used as a synonym for "all", as in Isaiah 53:11,12 and Romans 5:15,19. But that is not the case here. Whereas the majority will sign up, the saints of the Most High will see through the deception and will have no part in it. This agreement is "the covenant with death" described in Isaiah 28. The whole chapter should be read, but here are verses 14-22:

> Therefore hear the word of the Lord, you scoffers,
> who rule this people in Jerusalem!
> Because you have said, 'We have made a covenant with death,
> and with Sheol we have an agreement,
> when the overwhelming whip passes through,
> it will not come to us,
> for we have made lies our refuge,
> and in falsehood we have taken shelter';
> therefore thus says the Lord God,
> 'Behold, I am the one who has laid as a foundation in Zion,
> a stone, a tested stone, a precious corner stone, of a sure
>   foundation:
> Whoever believes will not be in haste.
> And I will make justice the line,
> and righteousness the plumb line;
> and hail will sweep away the refuge of lies,
> and waters will overwhelm the shelter.'
> Then your covenant with death will be annulled,

and your agreement with Sheol will not stand;

when the overwhelming scourge passes through,

you will be beaten down by it.

As often as it passes through it will take you;

for morning by morning it will pass through, by day and by
night;

and it will be sheer terror to understand the message.

For the bed is too short to stretch oneself on.

and the covering too narrow to wrap oneself in.

For the Lord will rise up as on Mount Perazim; (2 Samuel 5:17-
20)

as in the valley of Gibeon he will be roused; (2 Samuel 5:22-
25)

to do his deed - strange is his deed!

and to work his work - alien is his work!

Now therefore do not scoff, lest your bonds be made strong;

for I have heard a decree of destruction

from the Lord God of hosts against the whole land.

The usual construction is "to cut a covenant" as in Isaiah 28:15, but in Daniel "he shall make strong a covenant". This verb "make strong", in the form it is found here, occurs again only in Psalm 12:4: "May the Lord cut off all flattering lips, the tongue that makes great boasts, those who say, 'With our tongue *we will prevail*, our lips are with us, who is master over us?'."

The Antichrist will forge this covenant through flattery and double-talk. With his fine words he will convince the majority, with his tongue he will prevail. Leupold translates, "He shall make a covenant to prevail." Keil says, "he who concludes and confirms the covenant prevails and imposes or forces the covenant on the other party."

The view of E.J. Young and others that the covenant referred to here is the Covenant of Grace, on the basis of which life and salvation are freely offered to sinners, makes no sense in the context of this passage. As Pember says, "such a construction would violate grammar, logic, and the facts of history, and would throw the whole prophecy into confusion." This theory, says Sir Robert Anderson, "would deserve a prominent place in a cyclopaedia of the vagaries of religious thought."

And for half of the week

Commentators argue whether the correct translation is "for half of the week" as in the *ESV* or "in the midst of the week". Most of them seem to think that "in the midst" is more appropriate to the context, but the absence of "in" before "half" points rather in the opposite direction. *Hetsi* only means "midst" in the expressions "in the midst" (Exodus 12:29 etc.), "to the midst" (Exodus 27:5; Judges 16:3), and "from the midst" (Zechariah 14:4), as they appear in the orginal. Otherwise it always means "half". But it does not really make much difference which translation is adopted since what takes place in the middle of the week will certainly continue for the rest of the week.

The event which takes place in the midst of the week and continues throughout the concluding half-week (three and a half years) is the suspension of "sacrifice and offering". The words "sacrifice and offering" are mentioned in 1 Samuel 2:29 and Psalm 40:6. The totality of the Mosaic ritual is summed up by these words. The event referred to is the same as the taking away of the regular (offerings) in Daniel 8:11,12,13; 11:31 and 12:11. Coincident with the abolition of the Mosaic ritual will be the erection of the abomination of desolation (11:31; 12:11), called the transgression of desolation in 8:13, and the giving over of the sanctuary and host to be trodden under foot (8:13). Our present verse, 9:27, goes on to speak of these profanities.

And on a wing of the temple

"And on a wing (of the temple) he will set up an abomination that causes desolation." This is the *NIV* translation which follows the *Septuagint* and Theodotion. The words "of the temple" are absent from the Hebrew text but are probably implied. With no alteration of the consonants the Hebrew says, "and upon a wing abominations that cause desolation."

Abominations is plural here as if more than one abomination will be installed - which is not at all improbable. And by "the wing" is understood some projection or pinnacle of the Temple. This word is used widely of borders and extremities, especially of garments and the earth. It is not elsewhere used of any part of a building, but its Greek equivalent is used of an elevation of the Temple in Matthew 4:5 (=Luke 4:9). Montgomery says, "We may suppose a heathen image or emblem - an acroterion, to use the architectural term - set up by Antiochus upon the pediment or gable of the porch of the temple."

Acroterions are defined as "the pedestals, often without bases, placed on the centre and sides of pediments for the reception of figures." On one such pedestal (or more than one) the Antichrist may set up an idolatrous image, possibly of himself, which will outrage the Jews and cause deep offence.

The word "abomination" is regularly used of idols. In a single passage, 1 Kings 11:5-7, we read of Milcom the abomination of the Ammonites, Chemosh the abomination of Moab, and Molech the abomination of the Ammonites. The participle *meshomem* occurs elsewhere only in Ezra 9:3,4 in the sense of appalled ("I sat appalled"). But that sense is not suitable here. Keil thinks it means "the desolating abomination, i.e. the abomination which effects desolation." Another possibility is "appalling, causing horror" (BDB, *The Hebrew Dictionary*). The Greek equivalent *eremosis* means desolation, devastation. This word occurs in Luke 21:20, "But when you see Jerusalem surrounded by armies, then know that its desolation has come near."

In the singular "abomination of desolation" occurs again in Daniel 11:31; 12:11; 1 Maccabees 1:54; Matthew 24:15 and Mark 13:14. In the last passage it is construed with a masculine participle *hestekota*, standing. Not content with setting up a detestable idol in the Jerusalem Temple, the Antichrist will actually enthrone himself there, taking his seat in the Temple of God proclaiming himself to be God (2 Thessalonians 2:4).

Until the decreed end is poured out on the desolator

The phrase "decreed end" is exactly the same as in Isaiah 10:23 and 28:22, quoted above. In Isaiah 10:22 the wording is only slightly different. The verb "pour out" is frequently found with God as the subject and "wrath" as the object. Here God's wrath is poured out on the desolator, the one who has caused so much havoc and desolation.

Having discussed the various terms employed we are now in a position to consider how best to interpret the prophecy as a whole. The technical details may seem a little involved, so this part of the discussion has been deferred to Appendix 2. There will be found not only our own view, but those also of other schools of thought. For the moment it will suffice to state very briefly the fulfilment of the prophecy as seems right to us.

The entire prophecy of the Seventy Weeks, viewed in prospect, should have been fulfilled in 490 years, that is 70 weeks of years. These years however are not solar years but luni-solar or prophetic years of 360 days each. We are thinking therefore of 483 years rather than 490. (490 X 360 = 176400 divided by 365.25 = 482.95). The prophecy is divided 7, 62 and 1. After 7 weeks (48 solar years) Jerusalem would be built again with squares and moat. After a further 62 weeks (428 years) Messiah would be cut off. At the beginning of the last week of years the coming prince (the Antichrist) will make a strong covenant with "the many", but this covenant he will violate in the middle of the week. At this point he will put an end to "sacrifice and offering", and on a wing of the Temple (in Jerusalem) he will set up "abominations of desolation". This will be allowed to continue for the rest of the week, three and a half years (1260 days). This will be a time of great tribulation for the Jews, but at the end of the period the decreed end will be poured out on the desolator. Chronologically it looks as follows:

> After 7 weeks (445-397 BC): The city rebuilt
> After 62 weeks (397-AD 32/33): Messiah cut off
> After one more week: Antichrist is destroyed and everlasting
> righteousness comes in.

But the last week of years was postponed to a future time and still to this day has not been fulfilled. For a full explanation of this prophecy, and the different interpretations which have been proposed, the reader is referred to Appendix 2.

When did Israel cease to be God's people?

Many will agree with Sir Robert Anderson: "When wicked hands set up the cross on Calvary, and God pronounced the dread '*Lo-Ammi*' upon His people, the course of the prophetic era ceased to run" (p.86). Or G.H. Pember: "On the tenth day of the month Nisan (Palm Sunday), God gave up the sinful nation which had rejected His Son. His covenant was suspended, so that they were no longer His people" (p.345).

It is clear, however, that the dread *Lo-Ammi* ("Not My People") was not in fact pronounced at Calvary at all. To the contrary, the Jews were given a new lease of life while they reconsidered their verdict on the person of Christ. The Jews hold centre stage throughout the book of Acts, and were still "God's people" near the end of that period (Rom. 3:1; 9:1-6; 11:1). Moreover, the last week of years was still expected in the near future when the book of Revelation was written (Revelation 1:1; 22:10). We can only conclude that Daniel's seventieth week was postponed initially for one generation only, and it was only after Israel had failed once again to repent of their sin that the present intercalary age was interposed.

The New Testament epistles and Revelation, written during Acts, anticipate a resumption of prophecy in the very near future. It was only after that, when the Jews of the *diaspora* had shown themselves to be of the same disbelieving disposition as the Jews in the land, that a much longer postponement took effect. The Jews received their just deserts for rejecting their Messiah, and the gospel was given free rein among the Gentiles instead.

When will Israel assume centre stage again?

When will God take up Israel again? Will it be at the beginning of the last seven years, or earlier still when prophecy is resumed? Arguably, God has already taken up Israel in that they are once again a sovereign nation back in their own land. But Israel is not at present in covenant relationship with God, nor are they God's people in any real sense. They are indeed God's people in waiting, but the relationship has yet to be confirmed. That will not take place until after the tribulation when, at the second coming of Christ, the nation repents of its unbelief and the new covenant is established (Zechariah 12:10-13:1). Events will not reach a head until the second coming of Christ. That is when Israel takes over from the Church and the Church will appear with Him in glory (Colossians 3:4). It is at the *Parousia* that the rapture takes place, not seven years before (1 Thessalonians 4:15).

Daniel Ten

The Man Clothed in Linen

It was now the third year of Cyrus king of Persia, and Daniel once again was mourning and wrestling with the vision he had received. For three whole weeks he abstained from pleasant food, meat and wine, and from anointing himself with oil. He had much cause to be sorrowful. The invitation to the Jews to return to their homeland two years previously had met with a poor response. Only 43,000 had taken up the challenge, the rest preferring the relative comfort and security of exile in Babylonia. The command to rebuild Jerusalem, which he had expected in the first year of Cyrus, had not materialized. Even the command to rebuild the Temple, which had materialized, was not progressing well. In fact it was not progressing at all, thanks to the people of the land who had bribed the counsellors to frustrate the project (Ezra 4:4-5). Even that was now at a standstill. As Pember observes, "those who had returned were few, feeble, dispirited, and harassed on all sides by enemies, what marvel was it that the prophet fasted and mourned?"

There was another reason for Daniel's mourning, a more personal one. That was his lack of understanding, his failure to understand the vision of Daniel 8 (v.27), and possibly that of Daniel 9 as well. This is the reason given by the angel: "Fear not, Daniel, for from the first day that you set your heart to understand and humbled yourself before your God, your words have been heard, and I have come because of your words ... and I have come to make you understand what is to happen to your people in the latter days" (10:12,14). Daniel had prayed for understanding, and now the angel had come to give him understanding. Now, thanks to the angel's instruction, "he understood the word and had understanding of the vision" (10:1).

A man clothed in linen

On the 24th day of the first month, a day to be remembered, he had a vision of a glorious divine being, resplendent in beauty and dazzling with fiery light. As with Paul on the Damascus road, Daniel alone saw the vision. His companions were overcome with a great trembling and "they fled by hiding themselves" as the Hebrew graphically puts it (v.7). Daniel himself was completely sapped of all strength; he fell into a swoon with his face to the ground. As Berrigan puts it in his own inimitable way, "Up to now, Daniel is pure dazzle. No agony. No Gethsemane", but now "the visitation all but breaks his bones ... All told, he is one of us, mortal, and bearing the cicatrice (scar) of his high calling."

But this magnificent being was not the Lord himself. He had been "sent" (v.11) and needed the help of Michael, one of the chief princes (v.13). He was therefore but a mighty angel, Gabriel or some other. His appearance was similar to other glorified beings we read of in Scripture. He had the resemblance of a man clothed in linen, and this reminds us of the angelic being in Ezekiel 9 and 10: "the man clothed in linen, with a writing case at his waist" (9:2,3,11; 10:2,6,7). He appears again in Daniel 12:6-7. Daniel's angel did not have a writing case but "a belt of fine gold from Uphaz round his waist." This reminds us of the glorified Son of Man in Revelation 1:13, who had "a golden sash round his chest." Furthermore, his body was like beryl (*tarshish*), and his face like the appearance of lightning. These features remind us of the cherubim in Ezekiel 1:13,16 and 10:9.

His eyes were like flaming torches, as were those of the Son of Man whose "eyes were like flames of fire" (Revelation 1:14). His arms and legs like the gleam of burnished bronze. The same words are used of the cherubim in Ezekiel 1:7 and of the Son of Man in Revelation 1:15 whose "feet were like burnished bronze, refined in a furnace." The mighty angel of Revelation 10:1-3 had a "face like the sun, and his legs like pillars of fire."

"The sound of his words like the sound of a multitude." The last word means "a roar", whether of tumult or water. This again reminds us of the Son of Man whose "voice was like the roar of many waters" (Revelation 1:15); of the cherubim, whose wings were "like the sound of many waters, like the sound of the Almighty, a sound of tumult like the sound of an army" (Ezekiel 1:24); and of the God of Israel, the sound of whose coming was like the sound of many waters, and the earth shone with His glory (Ezekiel 43:2). The mighty angel of Revelation 10 "called out with a loud voice, like a lion roaring." We are left in no doubt at all as to the magnificence and exalted station of this angelic being. The angels are not the Lord in person; they are however like Him because they see Him as He is (1 John 3:2).

Daniel is in travail because of the vision

Just to be granted a vision of this nature, in spite of the weakness and sickness which followed, was a rare privilege. It was because Daniel was "greatly loved" (11,19), because he had applied himself to understand and to humble himself before God (12), and especially "because of your words", his prayers and confession, that the angel had been sent.

In verse 16 he says, "O my Lord, by reason of the vision pains have come upon me." Interestingly the same words are used of Eli's daughter-in-law in 1 Samuel 4:19. On hearing that the ark of God had been captured and that Eli was dead, "she bowed and gave birth, for her pains came upon her." Such was the intensity of Daniel's distress. The pangs of childbirth is the usual sense of this word (Isaiah 21:3; 13:8). The vision had been so overpowering that Daniel had been left speechless, breathless, sapped of all strength and aching all over. His pain was deep and abdominal as of a woman in labour.

Isaiah was similarly affected by his vision of the fall of Babylon in Isaiah 21:1-10. "Therefore my loins are filled with anguish; pangs have seized me, like the pangs of a woman in labour; I am bowed down so that I cannot hear; I am dismayed so that I cannot see" (21:3).

Angelic warfare

The angel for a moment draws back the curtain and tells Daniel what was going on behind the scenes all the time that Daniel was mourning. "The prince of the kingdom of Persia withstood me twenty-one days", he says, "but Michael, one of the chief princes, came to help me." But he has now come, he continues, "to make you understand what is to happen to your people in the latter days. For the vision is for days yet to come." He refers of course to the long revelation which occupies the whole of chapter 11.

Michael is "the great prince who has charge of your people" (12:1), that is Daniel's people, Israel. He is "your prince" (10:21), the archangel (Jude 9), the most powerful angel of all, the guardian angel of God's people Israel. He is here portrayed as helping the glorified angel now speaking in his struggle with the prince of the kingdom of Persia. With Michael's help this evil angel was subdued, and he "was left there with the kings of Persia." He was now able, it seems, to point the kings of Persia in the right direction whereas previously their own wicked prince had been manipulating them unopposed.

But the fight continues. "But now I will return to fight against the prince of Persia; and when I go out, behold the prince of Greece will come" (v.20). There is no let-up for the angel. For all his splendour and might, he is engaged in constant warfare with one prince after another. These princes cannot be called guardian angels, since guarding is a benevolent office. Their aim is to subvert, lead astray, to promote discord and injustice, and supremely to oppose God's purposes for Israel and the world. There is probably no nation on earth which is not influenced by its own malevolent angel, appointee of Satan.

As Berrigan well says, "Behind the wall that would hem us in, unaccountable and arrogant, guarding the realm of death, lurk the dynasts (*archoi*), the principalities. Clamorous and spurious both, they ape the spirits of God even as they oversee and govern the systems of the world. In this they are skilled indeed, buttressing, energizing, justifying, and rendering plausible the fallen creation, the structures given over to death. But these dark spirits hardly go unchallenged. Great angels, stand with us!"

It is true, they do not go unchallenged, nor do their satanic promptings have to be followed. Children also have their angels who constantly see the face of their Father in heaven (Matthew 18:10), and not only children (Psalm 91:11-12). But there are hordes of evil angels as well intent on doing mischief (1 Kings 22:19-23). Who can doubt that the horrific conflicts and tyrannies which have ravaged and plagued this world from time immemorial have been instigated by cosmic powers, "the spiritual forces of evil in the heavenly places" (Ephesians 6:12).

The climax

In the fullness of time the conflict in heaven will come to a head: Michael and his angels fighting against the dragon (Revelation 12:7). The dragon will be soundly defeated - that ancient serpent, who is called the devil and Satan, the deceiver of the whole world. He will be thrown down to earth, and his angels with him. The heavens will rejoice because the accuser of their brothers has been evicted. "But woe to you, O earth and sea, for the devil has come down to you in great wrath, because he knows that his time is short!" (Revelation 12:7-12). Then, quite literally, all hell will be let loose!

This time of wrath, and the events leading up to it, are the subject-matter of the scripture of truth which the angel was sent to reveal to Daniel. To that revelation we must now turn.

Daniel Eleven

Kings North and South and "the one Despised"

The revelation of future events begins at verse 2. It follows the same pattern as the vision of chapter 8 of which it may be regarded as an expansion. The kings of Persia are only mentioned in passing since that kingdom was now in power. We are however given some important information about these kings, information which has given rise to much argument and dispute. Verse 2 reads in the *ESV*, "Behold, three more kings shall arise in Persia, and a fourth shall be far richer than all of them. And when he has become strong through his riches, he shall stir up all against the kingdom of Greece."

He will stir up them all, the kingdom of Greece

The true interpretation hinges on the correct translation of the concluding words. Quite literally they say, "He will stir up the(m) all (namely) the kingdom of Greece." The verb translated "stir up", when followed by the preposition *eth*, as it is here, has the meaning to stir up someone or something. The word *eth*, as so often, introduces the definite object. When followed by the preposition *'al*, it means to stir up against, as in verse 25 of this chapter. There are several places where both prepositions occur in the same verse: 2 Chronicles 21:16 "The Lord stirred up against (*'al*) Jehoram (*eth*) the anger of the Philistines"; Isaiah 13:17 "Behold, I am stirring up against (*'al*) them (*eth*) the Medes"; Ezekiel 23:22 "I will stir up (*eth*) your lovers against (*'al*) you." In Daniel it is the whole kingdom of Greece which is stirred up or aroused.

A more precise elucidation of our verse is suggested by Franz Delitzsch's comment on Isaiah 7:17. He there says, "The particle *eth* is used frequently where an indefinite object is followed by the more precise and definite one (Genesis 6:10; 26:34)." In Isaiah 7:17 *eth* precedes "the king of Assyria", the more precise and definite object ("... *even* the king of Assyria"). In Genesis 6:10 it precedes "Shem, Ham, and Japheth." ("And Noah had three sons, *namely* Shem, Ham, and Japheth"). Likewise

Genesis 26:34, "and he (Esau) took a wife, *namely* Judith the daughter of Beeri the Hittite, and (*eth*) Bashemath the daughter of Elon the Hittite." The construction is the same in Daniel 11:2, "He will stir up all, *namely* the kingdom of Greece."

Commentators make heavy weather of this verse. Young says the construction is "extremely difficult", Leon Wood "problematic", Lucas "clearly elliptical ... difficult to construe", Montgomery "obscure". Only Montgomery is prepared to contemplate what is obviously the correct translation. He suggests, "and he will stir up all, namely (?) the kingdom of Greece."

The problem lies, not with the Hebrew construction, but with the interpretation presupposed by commentators. For them it is a foregone conclusion that the king referred to is Xerxes. Xerxes did stir up all his subject states against the king of Greece. Having made up their minds that the wealthy Xerxes is the fourth king of Persia, the translation has to be made to fit. Understandably, its refusal to do so has been a source of consternation and puzzlement!

How Daniel would have understood it

Commentators differ as to which four kings are referred to in verse 2. But that question cannot be answered without considering first how Daniel himself would have understood the vision. Daniel says that "he understood the word and had understanding of the vision" (10:1). If therefore we would aspire to do the same, Daniel is the one to ask.

Daniel was now in the third year of Cyrus, 534 BC by our reckoning. The command to restore and build Jerusalem which he had expected in the first year of Cyrus had not materialized. This would have been a matter of deep concern for Daniel, but he would doubtless have assumed that Cyrus would issue the command later in his reign, as indicated by Isaiah. There was no way he could have known that the command to rebuild Jerusalem would be delayed for another 89 years.

Daniel only knew what the revealing angel was permitted to tell him. He is told, "Yet three kings shall arise in Persia, and a fourth shall be far richer than them all." From this he could only have concluded that four more kings, and only four, would rule in Persia. Of these the fourth would be the richest by far, so much so as to attract the greed and cupidity of the kingdom of Greece. The fourth king, it is implied, would be overthrown by the kingdom of Greece, whose "mighty king" would take over his kingdom and himself "rule with great dominion and do as he wills" (v.3).

That is what Daniel would have expected to happen on the basis of what he had been told. That is how it could have been if the prospect had been fulfilled as revealed. But in practice it did not work out that way. Once again the human factor intervened to cause unexpected delays in the prophecy. It is only in retrospect that we can understand what really happened.

The four remaining kings of Persia

With the knowledge of hindsight, having some acquaintance with the facts of history, we naturally ask which four kings are intended. Commentators, almost without exception, assume that the three kings are Cyrus' immediate successors, Cambyses, Smerdis, and Darius Hystaspes. Some would include Cyrus himself whose reign had only just begun and would exclude Smerdis who reigned for only a few months. But there is general agreement that the fourth king is Xerxes who was certainly richer than his predecessors. Xerxes stirred up all against the kingdom of Greece, and was repulsed for his folly both by sea at Salamis (480 BC) and by land at Plataea (479).

But Daniel had been told "Yet three kings ... and a fourth." After Xerxes, however, there were still seven more kings to rule in Persia and a further 134 years after Xerxes' death before the conquest of the Persian Empire by Alexander the great. Montgomery stands almost alone in rejecting the common interpretation of Daniel. Xerxes, he says, cannot be the fourth (and last) king. "This is bald interpretation from Western history; that the Jewish tradition had any memory of Xerxes' wars with Greece it is absurd to conceive."

For Montgomery this chapter is historical reminiscence rather than predictive prophecy. But we may agree with him that Jewish prophecy is no more likely than Jewish tradition to take much notice of Xerxes' wars with Greece which had no bearing on Jewish history or the fulfilment of predictive prophecy. Montgomery prefers instead four representative kings: Cyrus, Xerxes and Artaxerxes, all mentioned in Ezra-Nehemiah, and Darius III, the last king of all. "It is no foregone conclusion", he says, "that this description must mean Xerxes, despite Esther and the Greek accounts of his marvellous wealth, e.g., Herodotus, VII, 20 ff. It was the wealth of Persia in the possession of its kings that astounded the world and aroused the lust of Alexander."

Montgomery's choice of kings may strike us as arbitrary, but at least he is on the right lines in regarding Darius III as the fourth and last king. Who, therefore, are the three kings who were yet to reign in Persia and the fourth who was far richer than them all? I quote from Sir Robert Anderson who understood the book of Daniel far better than most of his successors.

> The second verse is generally interpreted as though it were but a disconnected fragment of history, leaving a gap of over 130 years between it and the third verse, whereas the chapter is a consecutive prediction of events *within the period of the seventy weeks* [my italics]. There were yet to be (i.e., after the issuing of the decree to build Jerusalem) 'three kings in Persia'. These were Darius Nothus (mentioned in Nehemiah 12:22), Artaxerxes Mnemon, and Ochus; the brief reigns of Xerxes II, Sogdianus, and Arogus being overlooked as being what in fact they were, utterly unimportant and indeed two of them are omitted in the Canon of Ptolemy. 'The fourth' (and last) king was Darius Codomanus, whose fabulous wealth - the accumulated hoard of two centuries – attracted the cupidity of the Greeks. What sums of money Alexander found in Susa is unknown, but the silver ingots and Hermione purple he seized after the battle of Arbela were worth over £20,000,000 [a great deal more in today's money!]. Verse 2 thus reaches to the close of the Persian Empire; verse 3 predicts the rise of Alexander the Great; and verse 4 refers to the division of his kingdom among his four generals. (*The Coming Prince*, p.252)

I give here the names and dates of the Persian kings so that the reader can test for himself the soundness of Anderson's interpretation:

Cyrus II	559-530
Cambyses	530-522
Pseudo-Smerdis	522-521
Darius I Hystaspis	521-486
Xerxes I (Ahasuerus)	486-465
Artaxerxes I Longimanus	465-423
Xerxes II and Sogdianus	423
Darius II Nothus	423-404
Artaxerxes II Mnemon	404-359
Artaxerxes III Ochus	359-338
Arses or Arogus	338-336
Darius II Codomannus	336-331

It has already been observed that time is considered in Daniel only in so far as it falls within the 70 years of Babylonian rule (answering to the head of gold, Daniel 2) and the 70 Weeks of Daniel 9 (answering to the rest of the image, shoulders to toes). Anderson's interpretation is in line with that insight, only the four successors of Artaxerxes Longimanus being considered. Ideally the two periods should have followed on without a break. If Cyrus had been the one to restore and build Jerusalem, there would have been no gap and no break in the sequence of weeks. Cyrus however was not the one to sanction that event, nor was Darius whose decree (Ezra 6), like that of Cyrus, made no mention of the city. We find therefore that the head of the image was severed from its shoulders even in Daniel's lifetime. Later on the legs and feet were also to be severed, as we shall see. So much for Nebuchadnezzar's dazzling image!

A mighty king shall arise

"Then a mighty king shall arise, who shall rule with great dominion and do as he wills. And as soon as he has arisen, his kingdom shall be broken and divided towardsthe four winds of heaven" (11:3-4). There is no doubt that this mighty king is the first king of Greece who was enticed by the wealth of the crumbling Persian empire to invade and subdue that kingdom. Should there be any doubt, this is spelt out in chapter 8:21 where the he-goat is identified with the king of Greece, the great horn between his eyes being the first king.

Daniel himself would have known no more than this. But, with the knowledge of hindsight, all are agreed that Alexander the Great is the warrior-king of verse 3. His far-flung empire (from Egypt to the Indus and from Macedon to Samarkand), and his authoritarian rule, doing just as he pleases, are briefly touched upon. Alexander had barely risen to power when he was struck down by fever, just before his thirty-third birthday. He died in Babylon in 323 BC.

Ron Cantrill says of Alexander, "Like a comet, he lit up the sky, stringing conquered cities like pearls on a necklace: Troy, Ancyra (Ankara in modern Turkey), Tarsus, Sidon, Tyre (in modern Lebanon), Memphis (Cairo), Alexandria in the south; then on to Damascus, Opis (Baghdad), Babylon, Ecbatana, through Persia to the Far East - even as far as China." (p.126)

Towards the four winds of heaven

His kingdom, we are told, "shall be broken, and shall be divided towards the four winds of heaven." So also it was said of him in 8:8, "Then the goat became exceedingly great, but when he was strong, the great horn was broken, and instead of it there came up four conspicuous horns towards the four winds of heaven." His kingdom would pass "not to his posterity, nor according to the authority with which he ruled, for his kingdom shall be plucked up and go to others besides these" (v.4).

Alexander's heirs were not from his own family. Montgomery explains: "Alexander's stupid half-brother Philip Arrhidaeus, his posthumous son by Roxane, and an illegitimate son Herakles, who had been held as pawns by the would-be successors to Alexander, were done away with one after the other (in 317, 311, 309 respectively)." The actual succession was decided during the next twenty years, as R.H. Charles explains:

On the death of Alexander his empire became the curse of endless rivalries and wars amongst his generals, which raged over twenty years before a final settlement was arrived at through the battle of Ipsus in Phrygia in 301. By this settlement Egypt was confirmed to Ptolemy in the south; Asia Minor including Paphlagonia and Pontus to Lysimachus in the north; Seleucus received Syria and Babylonia, and other eastern provinces as far as the Indus in the east; Cassander, Macedonia and Greece in the west. These four new kingdoms rose on the ruins of Alexander's empire and are symbolized by the 'four horns'. (pp.202-3)

The concluding words translated "to others besides these" are taken to mean "besides the members of Alexander's family." But this is questionable since elsewhere the Hebrew *milevad* means "in addition to" rather than "to the exclusion of". Montgomery thinks we have here "a unique use of the phrase", but better is Young's explanation: "The meaning of the text probably is that in addition to the four-fold division, the kingdom shall belong also to others, namely, the petty dynasties which arose after the death of Alexander."

What would Daniel have expected?

Scholars are agreed that historically there was no new kingdom, answering to the fourth kingdom in Daniel 2, in 300 BC. H.H. Rowley says, "the succession states were ideally a single empire, which continued the empire of Alexander. Further, these states did not come into being by the conquest or overthrow of Alexander's empire, as the latter did by the overthrow of the Persians, or the Persians by the overthrow of its predecessors, but as a development out of it" (p.141). In point of might and dominion they were certainly much inferior to the empire of Alexander, as in fact is stated in 11:4 (and 8:22).

However, the question we should be asking is not what scholars think on the basis of history, but what Daniel would have thought on the basis of the words revealed to him. Daniel 11 is an expansion of Daniel 8. We read there that out of one of the four successor states of the goat kingdom there would arise a little horn, which grew exceedingly great towards the south, the east and the glorious land (8:9). This little horn is identified with the king of bold countenance, who understands riddles, who arises "at the latter end of their kingdom (the four successor states regarded as one), when the transgressors have reached their limit" (v.23). This king we found to be the same as the little horn of Daniel 7 and his kingdom the same as the iron-clay kingdom of Daniel 2. This is also what we find in Daniel 11: the contemptible person, verses 21-45, does the same despicable deeds as the little horns of chapters 7 and 8 and the coming prince of chapter 9. He comes moreover at the latter end of the kingdom of the North, the most important of the four successor states.

What therefore would Daniel have expected to happen? First he would have expected the Greek kingdom to divide into four lesser kingdoms, as in fact took place. He would then have anticipated another strong kingdom such as that predicted in 11:5, corresponding to the fourth kingdom of Daniel 2. At the latter end of that kingdom he would have expected the Antichrist to arise, as predicted in this chapter and chapter 8. There is also the time schedule to bear in mind. The Antichrist should have been the contemporary of Messiah according to Daniel 9. After only 483 years from the going forth of the command to rebuild Jerusalem both Messiah would be cut off and the Antichrist would make his 'covenant' with the many. Hence, Daniel would have expected the events of chapter 11:5-20 to bridge the gap between the partition of the kingdom of Greece and the rise of the Antichrist himself.

The abomination of desolation set up by the last King of the North (11:31) is the same as that set by the coming prince on a wing of the Temple (9:27). The abolition of the regular burnt offering in the same verse (11:31) is the same as that perpetrated by the little horn in 8:11-12 and the coming prince in 9:27. These events were still future when our Lord gave his prophetic discourse in Matthew 24 (see v.15). This proves that Antiochus Epiphanes cannot have fulfilled them in 167 BC. It also proves that the Seleucid kings prior to Antiochus Epiphanes are not the kings of the North predicted in Daniel 11. These kings are still future from verse 5 onwards. There was indeed a foreshadow of their career in the Seleucid kings, and another foreshadow in the Roman emperors up to and including Nero. But these kings did not fulfil the terms of the prophecy. We look therefore to a future series of kings in which this prophecy will find its true fulfilment. These are referred to in Revelation

17:10-11 where the Beast is said to be the eighth in a series of kings, just as Antiochus Epiphanes was the eighth king of the Seleucid dynasty.

The king of the South strong, but one of his princes stronger

"Then the king of the South shall be strong, but one his princes shall be stronger than he and shall rule, and his authority shall be a great authority" (11:5). The kingdom of the breakaway prince is described as great ("his dominion shall be a great dominion"). Almost the same words are used of Alexander's rule in verse 3: "he will rule (have dominion) over a great dominion." A completely new dominion meets us in 11:5, a kingdom equal in power and extent to that of Alexander. That kingdom has never yet been seen. True, Daniel would have expected it to arise after the partition of the kingdom of Greece. But in fact no new kingdom arose at that time as described in 11:5. What did occur was but a pale reflection of the kingdom yet to come.

The eight Seleucid kings culminating in Antiochus Epiphanes could never fulfil this prophecy: first, because the Seleucid monarchy was not a new and powerful kingdom like the fourth kingdom of Daniel 2; secondly, because Antiochus appeared 200 years ahead of schedule and was not the contemporary of Messiah; thirdly, because his career did not fall in the latter days which, according to 10:14, was the subject of the present vision; and fourthly, because the Seleucid kings have no prophetic significance and, so far as we are concerned, are of little interest or relevance.

Assuming however that Daniel 11 is future from the fifth verse onwards, "the chapter will yield instruction and vigour to saints who will go through the closing period of this age. They will be able to follow with exactness the political disturbances of the Near East, to recognize the advent of the Antichrist, to observe his rise and progress, and thus seeing these things come to pass men of faith will lift up their heads knowing that their redemption has drawn nigh (Luke 21:28)." (G.H. Lang, p.154.)

Many prophetic students are looking for the restoration of the Roman Empire. There, they think, in the countries of the European Union will be found the ten horns of the Beast. But they are looking in the wrong part of the world. It is not the restoration of the Roman Empire, but that of the Greek empire, the empire of Alexander the Great, for which they should be looking. Significantly, the countries mentioned in this chapter are those which encircled Israel - Persia, Greece, the North (Syria or Assyria), Edom, Moab, Ammon, Libya and Ethiopia. Neither Russia nor America comes within the orbit of this prophecy, let alone Rome and its affiliated countries.

Nebuchadnezzar's empire had potentially no boundaries. To him it was said, "the God of heaven has given the kingdom, the power, and the might, and the glory", and into his hands "he has given, wherever they dwell, the children of man, the beasts of the field, and the birds of the heavens," making him ruler over them all (2:37-38). This universal dominion was inherited by his successors. Alexander is said to have sighed because there were no more worlds for him to conquer! Writes A.E. Knoch, "Not since his time has there been an empire without a boundary. Rome was stopped in England and near the Rhine, and at the Euphrates." At is zenith the fourth kingdom will wield unlimited power. It will begin however in Syria-Iraq, the area north and east of Israel.

Interestingly, the kingdom of the South in this chapter is never called "Egypt", though Egypt is named three times in the prophecy (vs. 8,42,43), for Egypt is only a part of the kingdom of the South. D.M. Panton once expressed the view that the kingdoms of the North and the South "will rest strategically on Syria and Egypt, though themselves sweeping upward to the frozen Arctic and downward to the long wash of Australasian seas." (*The Panton Papers*, p.89).

That is rather an extreme view! It is nevertheless impossible to restrict the kingdoms of the South and North to Egypt and Syria. The only country called "The South" in the Bible is Sheba in South Arabia (Matthew 12:42; Luke 11:31), not Egypt at all. In Daniel 11 Egypt is certainly included, but probably most of north Africa and Saudi Arabia as well.

"The land of the North" in Jeremiah is Babylonia (e.g. 46:10, "the north country by the river Euphrates"), but it is not limited to Babylonia.

Babylon is itself laid waste by a nation from the north (50:3), and this nation is accompanied by many kings from the farthest parts of the earth (50:41). Beth-togarmah "from the uttermost parts of the north" (Ezekiel 38:6) was situated between the Black and Caspian seas. There is also a reference to "all the kings of the North far and near" (Jeremiah 25:26). The kingdom of the North will be the mightiest empire of all time. Who can say how far it will extend? It will not however embrace the whole northern hemisphere (except possibly in its final phase), since according to Daniel 7 it will share the world with three other kingdoms.

It may seem strange that the break in this chapter should occur so early. In chapter 9 there is no break at all until the close of the sixty-ninth week. It would be natural to expect a similar pattern in all the other chapters as well. That is, an unbroken run of events until the cutting off of Messiah, then the long interval, with only the rise and fall of the Antichrist held over to a time still future. That to be sure is what one would expect, but Daniel 11 simply refuses to conform to this pattern. The only historical fulfilment on offer petered out in the mid second century BC, and there is no way it can be prolonged for another two hundred years.

The Antichrist is the end-product of the fourth kingdom of Daniel 2, and the last king in a series of kings whose fortunes are sketched in Daniel 11. If this sequence had really begun in 300 BC with the partition of the kingdom of Greece, it would have continued until the time of Christ when the Antichrist was expected. That is what Daniel would have expected, the fulfilment in prospect. When however the events of the end-time were postponed, it was not just the Antichrist whose coming was delayed, but the entire series of kings of which he is the last; not just the feet and toes of the image, but the legs as well, since legs, feet and toes all belong to the same kingdom of iron. It is this kingdom as a whole which must run its course at some future date.

11:5: A great dominion is established

Returning to verse 5, what exactly does it teach? Tregelles expands the translation as follows: "And the (first) king of the south (i.e. Egypt, see verses 7,8) shall be strong, and one of his princes (shall also be strong); and he (the prince) shall be strong above him (the first king of the south), and have dominion; his dominion shall be a great dominion." According to Keil, "the thought is this: one of the princes of the king of the south shall attain to greater power than this king, and shall found a great dominion. That this prince is the king of the north, or founds a dominion in the north, is not expressly stated, but is gathered from v.6 where the king of the south enters into a league with the king of the north."

This is the next event of prophetic significance to take place on this planet, when the fourth kingdom of Daniel 2 rises suddenly to power and Prophecy, the sleeping giant, wakes from its age-long slumber. The historical fulfilment on offer provides but a pale reflection of events still future. This partial fulfilment in the Seleucid and Ptolemy kings of Syria and Egypt will be found explained in all the commentaries, and there is no need to repeat it here. The victims of Antiochus' repression must have found help and encouragement in what they believed to be the fulfilment of Daniel 11, but in detail there is no exact agreement between the events predicted and their supposed fulfilment. Here, for example, as Keil points out, Seleucus was not in reality one of Ptolemy's generals. He did indeed enter into a league with Ptolemy, and when war arose led an Egyptian fleet against his rival Antigonus. Keil notes about a dozen discrepancies between Daniel 11 and history, all of which adds weight to our thesis that the time of fulfilment has not yet arrived.

When the prophecy is fulfilled it will be recognised as such by those who are watching for it. It will begin the sequence of events which will come to a head with the rise to power of the contemptible person of verse 21. Everything will be fulfilled as written in this chapter. There will probably be long intervals during which nothing appears to be happening, and then the next cluster of events will happen in quick succession. Those who are watching will know how much of the prophecy has been fulfilled, and how much yet remains.

11:6: A marriage agreement ends in disaster

"After some years they shall make an alliance, and the daughter of the king of the south shall come to the king of the north to make an agreement. But she shall not retain the strength of her arm, and he and his arm shall not endure, but she shall be given up, and her attendants, he who fathered her, and he who supported her in those times."

At the end of the years, that is after some years (2 Chronicles 18:2), they shall join themselves (as in 2 Chronicles 20:35). The daughter of the king of the South will come to, that is be given in marriage to (Judges 1:14), the king of the North to make *meysharim*, rights or equitable conditions (Psalm 99:4). It will be an equitable agreement designed to put the alliance on a firm footing. But she will not retain the strength of the arm - the strength to carry out the aims of the agreement. Likewise the king of the South will not stand, nor his arm. She herself will be given up (handed over, 2 Samuel 20:21), along with those who brought her, he that begat her and the one who strengthened her.

This attempt to form an alliance by marriage will evidently fail completely. It will result in the humiliation and possibly death of the king of the South. The last word, "in (those) times", may well belong to the next verse, as in *RSV* and *NRSV*.

11:7-9: The king of the South prevails

"And from a branch of her roots one shall arise in his place. He shall come against the army and enter the fortress of the king of the north, and he shall deal with them and shall prevail. He shall also carry off to Egypt their gods with their metal images and their precious vessels of silver and gold, and for some years he shall refrain from attacking the king of the north. Then the latter shall come into the realm of the king of the south but shall return to his own land."

Out of the branch of her roots (cp. Isaiah 11:1), that is from the family of the king's daughter, in his place shall one stand up (that is, the king of the South). He will come against (invade, as in Genesis 32:8; Isaiah 37:33) the army and penetrate the fortress of the king of the North. He will do battle with them and prevail. Their religious effigies and objects of veneration, along with their treasures of silver and gold, he will carry off to Egypt. He will then, for some years, stand off from (refrain from attacking) the king of the North. The king of the North will try to retaliate, but will return to his land having achieved nothing.

11:10: His sons will overflow and pass through

"His sons shall wage war and assemble a multitude of great forces, which shall keep coming and overflow and pass through, and again shall carry the war as far as his fortress."

Verse 9 spoke of something done by the king of the North; here the action continues with the deeds of "his sons". The words "overflow and pass through" are applied to the Antichrist in verse 40. He there overflows and passes through the glorious land (Israel) with devastating effect. Israel, situated between the North and the South, cannot fail to suffer when the king of the North overflows and passes through. The same words are used of the overflowing River of the mighty Assyrian in Isaiah 8:8 and 28:15,18. In Daniel 11:10 they carry the war as far as the fortress of the king of the South. In verse 7 it was the other way round: the king of the South entered the fortress of the king of the North.

11:11-12: The king of the South will cause tens of thousands to fall

"Then the king of the south, moved with rage, shall come out and fight with the king of the north. And he shall raise a great multitude, but it shall be given into his hand. And when the multitude is taken away, his heart shall be exalted, and he shall cast down tens of thousands, but he shall not prevail."

The king of the South will be enraged or embittered (as in 8:7 of the he-goat) and he will go out and fight against the king of the North. And he (the king of the North) will raise a large army, but this army will be given into his hand (that of the king of the South). When this takes place, his heart (that of the king of the South) will be lifted up; he will cause myriads to fall, but he will not achieve any lasting advantage.

The repeated change of subject calls for rather careful reading. Some have thought it is the king of the South who will raise a great multitude in verse 11, but the fact that the king of the North, in verse 13, again raises a multitude, greater than the first, proves that the king of the North is meant in verse 11 as well. This chapter may seem long and involved, but when it begins to be fulfilled, it will become the most topical chapter in the entire Bible!

11:13: The king of the North raises another large army

"For the king of the North shall again raise a multitude, greater than the first. And after some years he shall come on with a great army and abundant supplies."

The king of the North will return, having raised an army more numerous than before. At the end of some years (lit. "at the end of the times, years") he will keep on coming (as in v.10) with a great army and abundant supplies, the equipment and provisions of war.

The expression "at the end of the times, years" is certainly unusual. "In the end of the years" in verse 6 is similar but without "times". Times would seem to imply the times appointed by God. Only when those times have concluded will the king be permitted to carry out his designs, but those times will in fact extend to years. The next verse begins "In those times", the ones just referred to.

11:14: Jewish militants will take premature action

"In those times many shall rise against the king of the south, and the violent among your own people shall lift themselves up in order to fulfil the vision, but they shall fail."

In those times, the ones consisting of years mentioned in verse 13, many shall rise up against the king of the South. Violent men (lit. "sons of breaking", cp. Ezekiel 18:10 "a son, a robber") from Daniel's own people will exalt themselves with a view to establishing vision (prophecy in general), but they will stumble and fall. The reference is to Israel's zealots who, wanting to realise their national aspirations, will rise up in their own strength ahead of God's plan, and will suffer for their headstrong intervention.

11:15-16: The king of the North will do as he wills

"Then the king of the north shall come and throw up siege-works and take a well-fortified city. And the forces of the south shall not stand, or even his best troops, for there shall be no strength to stand. But he who comes against him shall do as he wills, and none shall stand before him. And he shall stand in the glorious land, with destruction in his hand."

The king of the North will raise siege-works and will capture a fortified city ("city of fortifications", either fortified cities in general, or more probably one in particular). The forces ("arms") of the South will not stand, not even his choice troops will have the strength. He (the invader) who comes against the king of the South will do just as he pleases; no-one will stand against him. He will stand (as victor) in the land of Desire (as in 11:41 and 8:9). This name for the promised land is derived from Jeremiah 3:19 "an inheritance the most desirable of the nations"; Ezekiel 20:6,15 "(a land) flowing with milk and honey, desirable to all lands." See at Daniel 8:9.

The destruction he wreaks on the land of Desire will not be a full end, as the word is sometimes translated, but only that decreed as in 9:27.

11:17: The king of the North brings terms of an agreement

"He shall set his face to come with the strength of his whole kingdom, and he shall bring terms of an agreement and perform them. He shall give him the daughter of women to destroy the kingdom (lit. "to destroy *her*"), but it (or she) shall not stand or be to his advantage."

The king of the North will resolve to come with the might of his whole kingdom behind him, with the clear intention of gaining possession of the kingdom of the South. He will bring with him the terms of an equitable agreement, as in verse 6. He will give the king of the South the daughter of women to destroy her. This however is not the purpose of the agreement, but the result of this political marriage. She will not stand, nor will he (the king of the North) gain anything from the arrangement.

According to the *ESV*, the purpose of the union is to destroy the kingdom of the South. But there is no mention of this kingdom in the context. "Daughter" is the only feminine noun to which the suffix can refer. The situation is very similar to that of verse 6. There it was the king of the South who took the initiative; and the alliance, though well meant, ended in disaster both for the king and his daughter. Here the king of the North takes the initiative. He imposes an agreement on the king of the South, but nothing is gained by it either for him or for the lady in question.

11:18-19: The king of the North is checked and humiliated

"Afterwards he shall turn his face to the coastlands and shall capture many of them, but a commander shall put an end to his insolence. Indeed, he shall turn his insolence back upon him. Then he shall turn his face towards the fortresses of his own land, but he shall stumble and fall, and shall not be found."

The king of the North directs his attention, first to the coastlands many of which he captures, and then to the fortresses of his own land, but in neither enterprise is he successful. Along the coastlands a commander will put a stop to his insolence, while in his own land he will come to total ruin.

The general meaning is clear enough. There is however disagreement over the concluding words of verse 18. The words "he will cause his reproach/ disgrace to return to him" are derived from Hosea 12:14 which the *ESV* translates, "and (the Lord) will repay him (Ephraim) for his disgraceful deeds." It is the word translated "indeed" (*bilti*) which is the problem. "Besides", "save that" and "except" are all well established meanings. The probable sense is that this commander will not only put a stop to the king's insolence, but will cause it to recoil on the king's head.

11:20: A taskmaster is sent

"Then shall arise in his place one who shall send an exactor of tribute for the glory of the kingdom. But within a few days he shall be broken, neither in anger nor in battle."

Noges, exactor, is the word translated "taskmaster" in Exodus (3:7; 5:6,10, 13,14) and "oppressor" in Isaiah (3:12; 9:4; 14:2,4; see also 60:17). It is also translated "oppressor" in Zechariah 9:8: "no oppressor shall again march over them, for now I see with my own eyes." This is followed by the statement, "behold your king is coming to you; righteous and having salvation is he, humble and mounted on a donkey, on a colt, the foal of a donkey." It is implied that Israel will be oppressed by many taskmasters prior to the coming of their King.

This word can also mean "collect tax or tribute" where the context demands (Deuteronomy 15:2,3; 2 Kings 23:35). If this translation is preferred by scholars, it is because it agrees best with the presumed fulfilment. But this *noges* may well be a taskmaster or oppressor rather than an extortioner of taxes.

This king of the North will be broken "within a few days". The words imply a very short time as in Genesis 27:44 and 29:20. In the historical fulfilment he is supposed to correspond to Seleucus IV who reigned for twelve years (187-176 BC). This is an obvious discrepancy between the text of Daniel and the supposed fulfilment in ancient times.

11:21: A contemptible person shall arise

"In his place shall arise a contemptible person to whom royal majesty has not been given. He shall come in without warning and obtain the kingdom by flatteries."

In his place, the place of the one just mentioned, shall arise one despised (used of Christ in Isaiah 49:7; 53:3), on whom was not laid the honour of the kingdom (unlike Solomon on whom the Lord "conferred the honour of the kingdom", 1 Chronicles 29:25). He will come in without warning (stealthily, cunningly, as in 8:25) and grasp the kingdom by intrigue or flattery. Cunning, hypocrisy, deception and flattery will be his hallmark. The word flattery occurs again in verse 32, "He shall seduce with flattery those who violate the covenant." Here however (vs. 21 and 34) we have the reduplicated form for emphasis, *halaqlaqoth*.

Here begins the career of Antiochus Epiphanes according to the usual interpretation. But Antiochus Epiphanes is simply a forerunner of the Antichrist, one of many such forerunners. It is clear from what follows that the person here described is the same as the little horn of Daniel 7:8, the stern-faced king of 8:23, and the coming prince of 9:26. Antiochus anticipated his career in some respects, but increasingly their stories diverge. This is another pointer that Daniel 11 is future from the fifth verse onwards since there is no break in the prophecy: one king succeeds another until the Antichrist makes his appearance.

S.R. Driver remarks, "it is contrary to all sound principles of exegesis to suppose that, in a continuous description, with no indication whatever of a change of subject, part should refer to one person and part to another." On this basis he argues for one king from verse 21 to verse 45. There is indeed a new paragraph at verse 36 which could conceal a break in the prophecy. Many have assumed that the prophecy jumps forward at this point from the career of Antiochus to that of the Antichrist. But the events described in verse 31 (the profanation of the temple, the taking away of the regular offerings, and the setting up of the abomination that makes desolate) are so clearly those ascribed to the Antichrist that to assume otherwise is sheer folly. If verse 31 speaks of the Antichrist, as surely it must, so does the preceding narrative back to verse 21 since the deeds of the same king are described throughout.

The character of this future king will mirror that of Antiochus Epiphanes but to a much higher degree. William Campbell quotes an unnamed writer who describes this king in the following way:

> ... the last king of the north is not a lineal descendant of royalty, but owes the sceptre to a political ferment. Like many a hero of ancient and modern times, this man of prophecy pushes his way to prominence by an extraordinary combination of great qualities. The circumstances attending his elevation may be summed up as

follows:- first, the revolution; then, the plebiscite; then, the despot. He is a man of transcendent greatness, a master of craft and cunning; a general, a statesman, a man of irrepressible enterprise and unflinching courage, full of resources, and ready to look in the face a rival or a foe. From an obscure station, without the advantages which rank and wealth afford, by sheer force of his ambition and his talents, combined with favourable circumstances, he attains a position which for a time puts him before the world as the greatest monarch of all time. By his suavity he secures a small following and executes a *coup d'etat* which renders him master of the situation. Once in power, he disarms prejudice by personal magnetism; and, by exercise of a specious generosity, wins many adherents to his cause.

11:22-23: His rise to power

"Armies shall be utterly swept away before him and broken, even the prince of the covenant. And from the time that an alliance is made with him he shall act deceitfully, and he shall become strong with a small people."

Opposing forces, flood-like in size and ferocity, will be simply swept away before him and broken in pieces. Even a prince of the covenant will suffer in the same way. "Covenant" is used in this chapter of the covenant people (vs. 28,30,32. Cp. "covenant of people", Isaiah 42:6; 49:8). This prince or ruler of the covenant is most probably a ruler or captain of Israel.

The verb "to make an alliance" is used in verse 6 of an alliance between the kings of the South and the North. His rise to power is here described as first, an alliance, a non-aggression treaty perhaps, or an agreement with the ruling party; then, he will cunningly increase his majority and better his position, until supreme power is achieved with the help of a small band of devoted supporters. First, the revolution; then the plebiscite; then the despot!

It is interesting to compare Hitler's rise to power in the 1920's and '30's.

In 1928 he had but twelve seats in the Reichstag. In 1930 this became 107; in 1932, 230. By that time the whole structure of Germany had been permeated by the agencies and discipline of the Nationalist Socialist Party, and intimidation of all kinds and insults and brutalities towards the Jews were rampant ... Hitler on his side knew that to carry out his programme of German resurrection an alliance with the governing elite of the Reichswehr was indispensable. A bargain was struck, and the German army leaders began to persuade Hindenburg to look upon Hitler as eventual Chancellor of the Reich ... The Corporal had travelled far." (Winston Churchill, *The Second World War*, Book 1, pp.52,54)

11:24: He will scatter largesse in the provinces

"Without warning he shall come into the richest parts of the province, and he shall do what neither his fathers nor his fathers' fathers have done, scattering among them plunder, spoil, and goods. He shall devise plans against strongholds, but only for a time."

He will come unexpectedly (*beshalwah*, as in v.21) into the fattest and richest parts of the province and there do unheard of things, which none of his ancestors had done. Plunder and spoil, seized from the richest provinces no doubt, he will distribute liberally. He will then plot the overthrow of strongholds - but only for a time.

11:25-27: He will defeat the king of the South unfairly

"And he shall stir up his power and his heart against the king of the south with a great army. And the king of the south shall wage war with an exceedingly great and mighty army, but he shall not stand, for plots shall be devised against him. Even those who eat his food shall break him. His army shall be swept away, and many shall fall down slain. And as for the two kings, their hearts shall be bent on doing evil. They shall speak lies at the same table, but to no avail, for the end is yet to be at the time appointed."

Both sides will have a great army (*hayil gadol*), but that of the South will be "mighty beyond measure". Even so, the king of the South will be defeated, for "they will devise devices against him." As in verse 24, these devices will be malicious, scandalous allegations such as those devised by Haman against the Jews (Esther 8:3; 9:25).

Some of those who devise devices will be those who eat at the king's table. Even those he thought to be friends and eat his bread will lift up their heel against him (Psalm 41:9). This is why his army is swept away with great loss of life. The two kings will seek through feigned friendship to destroy one another. Politicians have always lied at the same table, but the Antichrist will be the most persuasive liar of them all. Nothing will come of it however, since the appointed time has not yet arrived.

Very similar are the words of Habakkuk 2:3, "For still the vision awaits its appointed time; it hastens to the end - it will not lie. If it seems slow, wait for it; it will surely come; it will not delay." True prophecy is inspired by an impetus to fulfil itself. Though it tarries, as certainly it will, it cannot prove false. Patience will be rewarded because its fulfilment cannot be delayed indefinitely. Habakkuk speaks of the (last) king of Babylon, the same person as Daniel.

11:28: His heart is set against the holy covenant

"And he shall return to his land with great wealth, but his heart shall be set against the holy covenant. And he shall work his will and return to his own land."

The Antichrist, his heart lifted up with success, will turn his attentions against the holy covenant, and will do his pleasure before returning to his own land. What he will do is not recorded, but as G.H. Lang says, "This is the first appearing of the dark cloud that shall blacken Israel's sky into deepest night, the first muttering of that final tempest that shall sweep away every refuge of lies."

By the holy covenant is meant the divine institution of the old covenant. As A.E. Knoch well says, "The holy covenant can refer to one only - that made by God with the holy people (12:7), whose holy city (9:24), was on

His holy mountain (9:16)." Daniel 9 speaks of a very different covenant, one far from holy, which the coming prince will make with the many.

11:29-30: The time appointed

"At the time appointed he shall return and come into the south, but it shall not be this time as it was before. For ships of Kittim shall come against him, and he shall be afraid and withdraw, and shall turn back and be enraged and take action against the holy covenant. He shall turn back and pay attention to those who forsake the holy covenant."

The appointed time has now arrived. It is the middle of the last week of years, the time when Antichrist puts an end to sacrifice and offering and sets up the abomination of desolation, as we read in verse 31. Prior to that he will march again against the South, but the outcome this time will be very different from that of his earlier invasion (vs.25-26). He will be opposed by ships of Kittim which will cut off his advance. The only other mention of ships of Kittim comes in Balaam's prophecy in Numbers 24:24: "Alas, who shall live when God does this? But ships shall come from Kittim and shall afflict Asshur and (afflict) Eber, and he too (the afflicter) shall come to utter destruction." There must, surely, be a close connection between these two references to the ships of Kittim.

Kittim is used of Cyprus and of lands beyond Cyprus. If Asshur and Eber refer respectively to the eastern and western Semites, with Israel among the latter, what Balaam predicted was the affliction of these lands by a naval power from the West. In the short term this power would humble Asshur and thwart his pretensions but ultimately would itself suffer defeat and destruction. In Daniel 11:30 this prophecy of Balaam's begins to be fulfilled. The Antichrist will be grieved, cowed and disheartened by these ships of Kittim, and then galvanised into furious revenge. The object of his rage will be primarily "the holy covenant" (Israel) which he may regard as responsible for this interference from the West. In order to carry out his wicked designs he will make common cause with those in Israel who forsake the holy covenant. In this camp there will sadly be many.

In Isaiah the Antichrist is called Asshur, "the Assyrian" (10:5; 14:25). He will himself be an eastern Semite; otherwise he could not be attacked by ships from the direction of Kittim. Those who say he will be Roman or European stumble at this verse.

11:31-32: He will profane the Sanctuary and take away the Continual

"Forces from him shall appear and profane the temple (and) fortress, and shall take away the regular burnt offering. And they shall set up the abomination that makes desolate. He shall seduce with flattery those who violate the covenant, but the people who know their God shall stand firm and take action."

If language has any meaning at all, the parallel statements in Daniel and the New Testament must be accepted as proof that the perpetrator of these acts can only be the Antichrist. It is however commonly believed that Antiochus Epiphanes still holds the stage until verse 36.

"Forces from him ... shall profane the sanctuary, the fortress, and shall take away the regular (burnt offering), and they shall set up the abomination that makes desolate." In Daniel 8:11 "From him (the Prince of the host) the regular (burnt offering) was taken away, and the place of his sanctuary was overthrown." In 9:27, "For half of the week he shall cause sacrifice and offering to cease, and upon a wing there shall be abominations that make desolate." In 12:11, "from the time that the regular (burnt offering) is taken away and the abomination that makes desolate is set up shall be 1,290 days." The testimony of Daniel is unanimous that these events are still future: Antichrist is the perpetrator, not Antiochus Epiphanes.

It is moreover to these verses (11:31 and 12:11) that our Lord makes reference in Matthew 24:15 (= Mark 13:14). By so doing He has given His stamp of approval to the above interpretation. As Tregelles says, "it is only in chap. xi.31 and in chap. xii.11 (which depends on it) that it [the abomination of desolation] is spoken of by the name which our Lord uses; to this vision, therefore, I believe that he distinctly refers, and this reference I take as a defined point in interpreting the prophecy" (p.182).

1 Maccabees 1:54 describes what was done on the orders of Antiochus Epiphanes: "they set up the abomination of desolation (*bdelugma tes eremoseos*, as in Matthew and Mark and the Greek texts of Daniel) upon the altar, and builded idol altars throughout the cities of Judah on every side." Likewise Josephus (*Antiquities*, XII,5,4), "And when the king had built an idol altar upon God's altar, he slew swine upon it." But this only proves that the writer of 1 Maccabees thought that Daniel was speaking of Antiochus, not that he really was (except in type). "The writer knew what had just befallen his nation in the reign of Antiochus Epiphanes; he knew, too, what Daniel had predicted, and he thought, naturally enough, that the one was the fulfilment of the other" (Tregelles, 181). The view that Antiochus fulfilled the prophecy is "disproved on the verbal ground that *canaph* [wing] cannot designate the surface of the altar" (Keil).

Those who violate the covenant, verse 32, he will seduce with flatteries. But the Hebrew word does not mean seduce, but "to desecrate, to make profane; and spoken of persons, to make them a heathen, as frequently in the Syriac" (Keil). How will he heathenize them? He will do so by causing them to forsake their customs and law including circumcision, and to behave in all respects as heathen. On the other hand, the people who know their God will stand firm and will act accordingly, refusing to be intimidated or coerced.

11:33-35: Some of the wise will stumble

"And the wise among the people shall make many understand, though for some days they shall stumble by sword and flame, by captivity and plunder. When they stumble, they shall receive a little help. And many shall join themselves to them with flattery, and some of the wise shall stumble, so that they may be refined, purified, and made white, until the time of the end, for it still awaits the appointed time."

The importance of wisdom and understanding is emphasized in Daniel 12:3,10 and Matthew 24:15. By means of their understanding the wise will be able to explain to the people the prophetic significance of what is going on and to encourage them to stand firm. They will however suffer for their faithfulness, as our Lord reiterated later on. "Then they will deliver you up to tribulation and put you to death, and you will be hated by all nations for my name's sake" (Matthew 24:9). "And brother will deliver brother over to death, and the father his child, and children will rise against parents and have them put to death. And you will be hated by all for my name's sake. But the one who endures to the end will be saved" (Mark 13:12-13).

They will receive a little help from some quarter not specified. But at the same time many will join them with flatteries (smooth, slippery, fine-sounding promises, the reduplicated form as in v. 21), with a view to undermining them from within. All this trial and tribulation has one end in view, to refine, purify and make them white. The same three verbs are repeated in Daniel 12:10, "Many shall purify themselves and make themselves white and be refined, but the wicked shall act wickedly. And none of the wicked shall understand, but those who are wise shall understand."

All this will go on "until the time of the end, for it still awaits the appointed time." Compare verse 27, "for yet the end (will be) at the appointed time." One appointed time had arrived in verse 29, the time for taking action against the holy covenant and for profaning the temple fortress. But the time of the end was still to come. Similar language is used in Daniel 8: "for at the time of the end is the vision" (v.17); "I will make known to you what shall be at the latter end of the indignation, for (it refers) to the appointed time of the end" (v.19). Not till 11:40 does "the time of the end" finally arrive, but everything that precedes presses on resolutely in that direction. To that end all Daniel's visions strain forward uncompromisingly.

11:36: The king shall do as he wishes

"And the king shall do as he wills. He shall exalt himself and magnify himself above every god, and shall speak astonishing things against the God of gods. He shall prosper till the indignation is accomplished; for what is decreed shall be done."

According to Keil, "*Ham-melech* (the king) with the definite article undeniably points back to the king whose appearance and conduct are described in verse 21-33." But there is also truth in the statement, "The vile person of v.21 - ambitious, not always successful, experiences a mighty change when Satan energises him. He becomes 'The King'" (William Campbell).

Certainly from this point onwards he is invincible and supreme (till the indignation is accomplished), but the change from contemptible person to Satanic monster will have already taken place "at the time appointed" (v.29). If the talking image of Revelation 13 is the same as the abomination of desolation, his sword-wound must have already been healed before verse 31. There is much that we now understand (from the book of Revelation) that was not revealed to Daniel.

Antiochus wanted the worship of Zeus to be made universal. The Antichrist however will stop at nothing. It is he "who opposes and exalts himself against every so-called god or object of worship, so that he takes his seat in the temple of God, proclaiming himself to be God" (2 Thessalonians 2:4). "Who is the liar," asks John, "but he who denies that Jesus is the Christ? This is the antichrist, he who denies the Father and the Son" (1 John 2:22). He will indeed speak astonishing things against the God of gods. His boastful utterances are mentioned three times in Daniel 7 (8,11,20). Other blasphemers have denied the existence of God; only he will set himself up in the place of God.

He will prosper until (but only until) the indignation is ended - 'ad kalah za'am. Compare chapter 8:19, "the latter end of the indignation". We have here another allusion to Isaiah. Isaiah 10:25, "In a very little while the indignation shall cease (kalah za'am)"; 26:20, "Come, my people, enter your chambers, and shut your doors behind you; hide yourselves for a little while until the indignation has passed by." The indignation is the day of wrath, the day of judgment. It is especially God's indignation against Israel which is meant, though the nations are also included (Zephaniah 3:8; Habakkuk 3:12; Revelation 6:17 etc.).

11:37-38: He will honour the god of fortresses

"He shall pay no attention to the gods of his fathers, or to the one beloved by women. He shall not pay attention to any other god, for he shall magnify himself above all. He shall honour the god of fortresses instead of these. A god whom his fathers did not know he shall honour with gold and silver, with precious stones and costly gifts."

For some writers "God of his fathers" has a Jewish ring about it. E.J. Young for example: "The phrase has a Jewish emphasis and has reference to the Jewish religion. The man who has no regard for this Jewish religion is himself a Jew, the Antichrist." But if that were the case we might expect "the God of *our* fathers". The translation "gods of his fathers" is more probable in view of the fact that "god" is plural here, but singular in verses 37b, 38 and 39. It is true, to be accepted as their Messiah by the Jews, he will have to convince them that he is a bona fide Jew himself; but being the master of lies and deception the evidence he produces may well be false. It is by no means certain that he will really be a Jew. But if he is the one who comes in his own name, the Jews will certainly receive him (John 5:43).

"Nor unto the desire of women" - this is another phrase which has given rise to much speculation. For the meaning of the words compare 1 Samuel 9:20, "To whom is all the desire of Israel?" That is, Whom does Israel desire? Or Haggai 2:7, "the Desire of all nations shall come" (*KJV*). That is, the One desired by all nations. Hence it is some thing or person desired by women which is referred to, not the subjective desire *for* women.

Many would interpret this of Tammuz-Adonis, the queen of heaven, bearing in mind that it was women in particular who mourned for Tammuz (Ezekiel 8:14). On this view he will have no use for sentimental religious beliefs such as (some) women find attractive. Others think that the need for love and affection is the chief desire of women. This man will be without natural affection (Romans 1:31; 2 Timothy 3:3). Both women and religion will seem to him weak and despicable, and all such he will scornfully reject. His celibate life-style, single-minded determination, and overweening megalomania will leave no room for natural affection of any kind.

According to others (Gaebelein, Walvoord) the desire of women is that most desired by all Jewish women, namely to be the mother of the Messiah, hence the Messianic hope in general. But Christ is the Desire of all nations, not specifically of women, and the messianic hope is by no means confined to women. In point of fact the Antichrist will have a keen regard for the messianic hope since he himself will claim to be the Messiah, and this hope he will manipulate to his own advantage.

In favour of the first alternative is the passive turn of the phrase: that desired by women, and the fact that the context dwells exclusively on religion. Pember has this to say:

> The expression, "the Desire of Women," is placed between two nouns which indubitably refer to concrete gods; it must, therefore, itself designate some individual deity which is more especially sought after by women. And having reached this point, our difficulties are over: the deity intended can be no other than the many-named Goddess of Nature, who has been worshipped, and at all times chiefly by women, from the earliest ages to our own days, by Pagans and by apostate Christians of every land. She is the Beltis, or Mylitta, of the Babylonians; the Ishtar of the Assyrians; the Astarte of the Phoenicians; the Queen of Heaven mentioned by Jeremiah; the Tanata of the Persians; the Isis of the Egyptians; the Shing Moo, or Holy Mother, of the Chinese; the Aphrodite of the Greeks; the Artemis, or Diana, of the Ephesians; the Venus of the Romans; the Friga of the Scandinavians; the Amida, with her son Xaca, whom Francis Xavier found established as the goddess of Japan; the woman presented for worship by Strauss, Comte, and the Theosophists; and the Virgin Mary of the Eastern and Western Catholics. (p.428)

The same thought is taken up in the next verse. He will honour a god which his fathers did not know, namely the god of fortresses. As Leon Wood remarks, "the thought is that he will find his goal in fortresses, strongholds, and military programs, in place of such religious belief ... Military activity will take the place of god for him." Thus, in the place of any god he will honour war as his god. "For religion he will substitute war, and war he will support with all that he has" (Young).

11:39: Those who acknowledge him he will load with honour

"He shall deal with the strongest fortresses with the help of a foreign god. Those who acknowledge him he shall load with honour. He shall make them rulers over many and shall divide the land for a price (or, as payment)."

With the aid of the strange god aforementioned, namely the god of fortresses, he will conquer the strongest fortresses. Those, and only those, who acknowledge him (in obsequious adoration) will he reward. These he will heap with honour and land. They will be given (at a price) the rulership over conquered nations, which they will govern as puppet rulers in his name and at his behest.

11:40: He will overflow and pass through

"At the time of the end, the king of the south shall attack (Hebrew, thrust at) him, but the king of the north shall rush upon him like a whirlwind, with chariots and horsemen, and with many ships. And he shall come into countries and shall overflow and pass through."

Hitherto the end-time has been spoken of as still future (11:27,35). Here however, at long last, the time of the end has arrived. The remaining verses describe what will transpire at the end, the very last events before the second coming of Christ.

With this verse and the following, Isaiah 8:6-8 should be compared, for there we find the origin of the phrase *shataph we'abhar*, overflow and pass through. We have already encountered these words in Daniel 11:10 where they are used of an earlier king of the North. According to Isaiah 7:18-19 the Assyrian and Egyptian armies will clash on Palestinian soil. The Assyrians will be victorious and will devastate and denude the Holy Land (7:20-25). This prophecy will be fulfilled in the middle of the last week of years. It would seem that another hurricane-force invasion will overwhelm these lands at the time of the end.

His coming like a whirlwind may be another allusion to Isaiah. In Isaiah 28:2 the Lord has one who is strong and mighty. This one comes like a storm, a destroying tempest (or whirlwind), like a storm of mighty overflowing waters, and treads under-foot the proud crown of the drunkards of Ephraim. "Then your covenant with death [that of Daniel 9:27] will be annulled, and your agreement with Sheol will not stand; when the overwhelming scourge passes through, you will be beaten down by it" (28:18). Here also the words "overflow" and "pass through" are found.

But will this end-time battle be fought with horses and chariots? This is a question which applies to many other prophecies besides this one. In Ezekiel 38:4 for example the forces of Gog are equipped with horses and horsemen, and are clothed in full armour with bucklers, shields and swords. Likewise in Zechariah 14:15, horses and mules, camels, donkeys and other beasts are employed in the last battle of all. Surely no future battle will be fought in this manner.

The answer must lie in the fact that the prophets of old were not thinking in terms of modern warfare. The chronological limit of Daniel's visions is the first century AD when the seventy weeks were due to expire. He did not foresee the extended delays which his programme would subsequently sustain through the unbelief of later generations of his people. The prophets could not have foreknown that their predictions would be postponed for hundreds of years beyond the chronological horizon revealed to them. This huge delay arose because Israel as a nation rejected their Messiah, something which none of the prophets was given to understand.

If their prophecies had been fulfilled at the time expected, they would doubtless have been fulfilled in the manner described. But in view of the long delay, should we not update these prophecies in terms of modern warfare? For horses and chariots we should substitute their modern equivalents, tanks and armoured vehicles; for shields and swords we should think of rockets and missiles, etc. Kings may turn out to be presidents, and ships to be nuclear submarines. Likewise, for Edom, Moab and Ammon in the next verse we should substitute their modern equivalents. This future battle will not be fought with bows and arrows;

it will be the most sophisticated war this planet has ever experienced. The devil will marshal every weapon in his arsenal in order to wipe Israel off the map.

11:41: He will invade the glorious land

"He shall come into the glorious land. And tens of thousands shall fall, but these shall be delivered out of his hand: Edom and Moab and the main part of the Ammonites."

The Glorious Land, as in 11:16 and 8:9. The Hebrew has "many" (feminine plural), but by the change of a vowel-sign it can be turned into "myriads" or "tens of thousands", which makes better sense. Edom, Moab and Ammon are today's kingdom of Jordan to the SE of Palestine. The reason for their deliverance lies in their enmity for Israel. They find favour with the Antichrist because of their implacable hatred of the Lord's people. As it was in the days of Antiochus, the Arab nations will take counsel to destroy the race of Jacob in the midst of them (1 Maccabees 5:2). This was because they had "heard that the altar was built, and the sanctuary dedicated as aforetime." The rebuilding of the Temple in Jerusalem is bound to provoke the same reaction in the future.

11:42-43: All the precious things of Egypt will be his

"He shall stretch out his hand against the countries, and the land of Egypt shall not escape. He shall become ruler of the treasures of gold and silver, and all the precious things of Egypt, and the Libyans and the Cushites shall follow in his train."

No country will be able to stand against this frenzied attack. Not only Palestine, but the countries of north Africa will be powerless to resist. Persia, Cush (ancient Ethiopia, south of Egypt) and Put (Libyan region west of Egypt) are mentioned as siding with Gog in Ezekiel 38:5. They will willingly join forces with Gog, another name for the Antichrist, in his attempt to annihilate Israel.

11:44-45: He will come to his end with none to help

"But news from the east and the north shall alarm him, and he shall go out with great fury to destroy and devote many to destruction. And he shall pitch his palatial tent, between the sea and the glorious holy mountain. Yet he shall come to his end, with none to help him."

While he is absent in distant Africa, alarming news will reach him from the east and the north, China and Russia perhaps. In response he will plunge into another furious orgy of destruction. "Again will the Near and Middle East be deluged with blood as this mightier monster than a Jenghis Khan or a Tamerlane rages around" (G.H. Lang).

He will pitch the tents of his pavilion (*appadno*, a Persian word meaning "hall of honour") between seas and the Mount of Holy Delight, and (there) he will come to his end with no-one to help him" (cp. 8:25 "broken without hand"). His helpless end is spelt out in Isaiah 30:33 and Revelation 19:20. But how do we understand the words "between (the) seas and the mount of holy delight"?

There are two possible translations of these words. They can either be translated as above, or "between (the) seas, at the glorious holy mount". The latter has a respectable pedigree (*Theodotion, Syriac, Vulgate, KJV, RV* margin, *NIV* etc.), but grammatically it is less acceptable. The Hebrew construction is one of two common idioms for "between ... and". It is for example the same as in Genesis 1:6 "between waters and waters", and Joel 2:17 "between the porch and the altar."

With most moderns, therefore, we accept the translation "between (the) seas and the glorious holy mountain." By the mount of holy delight Mount Zion is meant, but what is meant by "seas"? It is generally assumed that the Mediterranean is meant, and that "seas" is the plural of extension or fullness. But the Mediterranean is never called by this name: it is either "the Sea" or "the Great Sea", never "seas". The reference could refer to any expanse of water, and the indications are that the Antichrist will meet his end in the vicinity of the Dead Sea - between the Dead Sea and Jerusalem.

The great end-time battle will take place in the vicinity of Jerusalem (Zechariah 12:1-9), outside the city (Revelation 14:20), in my land and on my mountains (Isaiah 14:25), on the mountains of Israel in the open field (Ezekiel 39:4-5), in the valley of Jehoshaphat ("multitudes, multitudes, in the valley of decision", Joel 3:2,12,14). A location near the Dead Sea may be indicated by the valley of Jehoshaphat. If this is an allusion to King Jehoshaphat's famous victory over Moab, Ammon and the inhabitants of Mount Seir (2 Chronicles 20), we are thinking of the wilderness of Tekoa, near Engedi on the west coast of the Dead Sea. In addition, Gog's hordes will be buried in "the Valley of the Travellers, east (or in front of) the (Dead) Sea" (Ezekiel 39:11). Their last act before being cut down like a forest will be to shake the fist at the mount of the daughter of Zion, the hill of Jerusalem (Isaiah 10:32). And this they will do at Nob, between Jerusalem and Anathoth, a few miles to the NE of Jerusalem. Hence the evidence points to some location very near to Jerusalem, between Mount Zion and the Dead Sea.

Conclusion

This prophecy is unique among prophecies, by far the longest and most detailed in the entire Bible. Either it is the record of events long past, events of little interest or value to believers today, or it is an invaluable forecast and preview of events still future, events which may begin to be fulfilled within the lifetime of some of us. There are many pointers in Daniel itself that the latter is the correct interpretation. As soon as the sequence begins to unfold there will be no difficulty in following it step by step to its dire conclusion. Those who have understanding will know exactly where they stand in relation to the run-up to the second coming of Christ. This will concentrate the mind most wonderfully as well as provide a powerful testimony to the world outside.

Daniel Twelve

The Time of the End

Daniel 12 continues straight on from the previous chapter as the opening words "At that time" go to show. These words are uttered three times in this verse, the time being "the time of the end" (11:40). In this crisis Michael is quick to intervene in defence of his people. He is here described as "the great prince who has charge of your people" (compare "Michael your prince", 10:21). In Revelation 12:7 he is seen again fighting against the dragon, described as "the accuser of our brothers ... who accuses them day and night before our God" (12:10). Michael therefore is the great prince appointed to be Israel's guardian.

His intervention is to be expected at this time when his people are in the worst trouble ever experienced since Israel became a nation, or any nation for that matter (v.1). It is the time of Jacob's trouble mentioned in Jeremiah 30:7. "Alas! That day is so great there is none like it; it is a time of distress for Jacob; yet he shall be saved out of it." As we have already been told, when Antichrist comes into the glorious land tens of thousands shall fall (11:41). Nevertheless, Daniel is assured, "your people shall be delivered, everyone whose name shall be found written in the book." There are references to this book in Exodus 32:32-33, Psalm 69:28, Isaiah 4:3 and Malachi 3:16. There are also six references in Revelation to the book of life of the Lamb slain (3:5; 13:8; 17:8; 20:12,15; 21:27). See also Luke 10:20, Philippians 4:3 and Hebrews 12:22-23.

Many of those who sleep shall awake

The angel goes on to speak of the resurrection of those who sleep, both the just and the unjust. "And many of those who sleep in the dust of the earth shall awake, some to everlasting life, and some to shame and everlasting contempt" (12:2). There are a number of important points which arise in connection with this statement.

(1) The resurrection is apparently selective. There are not a few places where "many" and "all" are practically synonymous terms (Matthew 20:28 "a ransom for many"; Matthew 26:28 "the blood of the covenant poured out for many"; Romans 5:15-16 "For if many died through one's man trespass, much more have the grace of God and the free gift ... abounded for many"), but here it is followed by the partitive "from". Not "multitudes who sleep" (*NIV*), but "many of those who sleep" (*ESV, NRSV*). It is therefore only some of those who sleep who will be raised at this time.

A similar situation occurs in Revelation 20:4 with reference to the first resurrection, the same as in Daniel. "I saw the souls of those who had been beheaded for the testimony of Jesus and for the word of God, and who had not worshipped the beast or its image and had not received its mark on their foreheads or their hands. They came to life and reigned with Christ for a thousand years."

We know from other passages (1 Corinthians 15:23; 1 Thessalonians 4:16) that all who belong to Christ will rise at this time, but John singles out for special mention those in whom he is particularly interested, those who are beheaded for their faithful witness during the tribulation period. It is the same in Daniel. Only those are mentioned with whom the angel is currently concerned, without necessarily denying that others will be raised as well.

(2) Those who sleep in the dust of the earth shall awake (literally, "earth of dust" or "dusty earth"). There is an allusion to Genesis 3:19 where earth (ground) and dust are both mentioned ("till you return to the earth ... for you are dust, and to dust you shall return"). Sleep is the usual euphemism for death, not because the two states are identical but because of the features they have in common, namely a state of unconsciousness followed by an awakening to renewed life. See also Isaiah 26:19 for an explicit mention of resurrection somewhat earlier than Daniel.

(3) Some to everlasting life and some to shame and everlasting contempt. This is the clause which has attracted the most attention, especially from premillennial writers who are unhappy with the idea of a double resurrection, some to life and some to shame, before the

millennium begins. According to Tregelles (p.164), the word twice rendered "some" is never repeated in any other passage in the Hebrew Bible, in the sense of taking up distributively any general class which had previously been mentioned.

It is not true however that *'elleh ...we' elleh* (some ... and some) is never used distributively in the Hebrew Bible. A few examples of this construction are the following: Joshua 8:22 "And the others came out from the city against them ...*some* on this side, and *some* on that side"; Psalm 20:7 "*Some* (trust) in chariots and *some* in horses, but we trust in the name of the Lord our God"; Deuteronomy 27:12-13 "*These* shall stand on Mount Gerizim ... *and these* shall stand on Mount Ebal." In each case the two companies belong to the same class of person, just as those in Daniel all belong to the same class, those raised from the dead.

There is nothing in Daniel to suggest that two resurrections are meant, one at that time and another at a later time. Yet we know from Revelation 20:5 that in point of fact the rest of the dead will not come to life until the thousand years are ended. Daniel, it would seem, speaks in general terms of the two resurrections without distinguishing between them in point of time. His after all was only a partial disclosure of future destinies sufficient for that time. We should not expect a complete revelation at the first mention of a subject.

Even our Lord spoke in general terms, making no distinction in time between the two resurrections. John 5:28-29: "Do not marvel at this, for an hour is coming when all who are in the tombs will hear his voice and come out, those who have done good to the resurrection of life, and those who have done evil to the resurrection of judgement."

(4) In Daniel 12:2 we have the first and only mention of "eternal life" in the Old Testament. The word for shame (*charaphoth*, reproaches, the plural of intensity) occurs elsewhere only in Psalm 69:10(9); and the word for contempt (*dera'on*) only in Isaiah 66:24, the last verse of that book. It means "loathsome, abhorrent", and is there applied to the dead bodies of the rebels: "their worm shall not die, their fire shall not be quenched, and they shall be an abhorrence to all flesh." The time is the beginning of the Messianic age, but no resurrection is mentioned in this

place, only the loathsome spectacle of their decomposing bodies.

The wise shall shine like the brightness of the sky (12:3)

The wise (*ha-maskil*) are mentioned also in 11:33,35 and 12:10. They are the ones who understand, and because they understand they are able to instruct also (11:33). In resurrection they will shine like the brightness of the heavens above, while those who turn others to righteousness will shine like the stars for ever and ever. In similar vein our Lord promised that the righteous will shine like the sun in the kingdom of their Father (Matthew 13:43). As Leon Wood comments, "The thought is that each of the 'wise' would shine like a star in the vastness of space."

There are also thirteen Maskil psalms whose purpose is to convey understanding. Of these six are by David (32,52,53,54,55,142), three by the sons of Korah (42,44,45), two by Asaph (74,78), one by Heman the Ezrahite (88), and one by Ethan the Ezrahite (89).

Shut up the words and seal the book (12:4)

Daniel is now instructed to "shut up the words and seal the book, until the time of the end." In like manner he had been told in 8:26 to "seal up the vision, for it refers to many days hence." In stark contrast are the instructions given to the apostle John who is told, "Do not seal up the words of the prophecy of this book, for the time is near" (Revelation 22:10). Very few writers attempt to explain why, in the case of two prophets of a similar kind, both relating to the time of the end, one should be sealed and the other remain unsealed.

The reasons are in fact given in the text. Daniel was to be sealed because the vision was not for many days, Revelation unsealed because the time of fulfilment had arrived. The time for fulfilment had also arrived for Daniel by the first century AD according to its own chronological limits (490 years). Both prophetic books were due to be fulfilled in the first century, and could have been so fulfilled if only the conditions had been met, namely the repentance and conversion of the people (Israel) who are central to both.

Revelation is in agreement with the other New Testament books written at that time, that the point of fulfilment had arrived, was even at the doors. If it did not happen, the reason is clear: the opportunity was forfeited through persistent unbelief. For the same reason Daniel's last week of years was cut off from the previous weeks and postponed to a future time, because the Jews refused to accept the Lord Jesus as their Messiah. The net result is that both prophecies reverted to the state of being sealed, and have remained so until recent times. In the fact that the message is now fairly well understood (if we are not deceiving ourselves), we may have a significant pointer that the time of fulfilment may not be too far away.

Many shall run to and fro

The next thing to be mentioned is, "Many shall run to and fro, and knowledge shall increase." The words themselves do not present any problem. They tell us what will take place at the time of the end or during the intervening period. To some extent this is what man has always done from Daniel's day to the present time. They are in fact a remarkably accurate forecast of the times in which we live. The unremitting quest for knowledge, coupled with ever further and faster travel, sums up the spirit of the age.

Sir Isaac Newton (so Campbell records) expressed the view that "men will yet travel on the earth at the rate of fifty miles an hour," for which modest prediction he was ridiculed by Voltaire half a century later. Lord Tennyson once wrote, "Science moves but slowly, slowly, creeping on from point to point." How things have changed in our generation!

The verb *shut* (in the Polel and Hithpolel conjugations) means to run about. It is used of running up and down the streets of Jerusalem (Jeremiah 5:1); of wandering from north to east (Amos 8:12); of the eyes of the Lord ranging through the earth (2 Chronicles 16:9; Zechariah 4:10); and of rushing hither and thither inside the walls (or among the hedges) of Rabbah (Jeremiah 49:3).

Many have seen an allusion here to Amos 8:12, "They shall wander from sea to sea, and from north to east; they shall run to and fro (*yeshotetu*, as in Daniel), to seek the word of the Lord, but they shall not find it." Here we have the other side of the coin, a frantic search for the word of the Lord, but one which meets with no success. Those who run to and fro in Amos fail in their quest, whereas those in Daniel are remarkably successful. Sadly, there are many today searching far and wide for knowledge of the Divine, but because they are looking in the wrong places they seem never to find Him.

How long?

Two more angels now appear, one on either side of the Tigris, while the angel clothed in linen hovers between them "above the waters of the stream." He is asked by one of the two angels, "How long shall it be till the end of these wonders?" The angel clothed in linen raised both hands to heaven and swore by Him who lives for ever and ever, that it would be for a time, times and half a time, by which time, it is implied, "the shattering of the power of the holy people comes to an end", and everything will be fulfilled.

These three and a half times are those of Daniel 7:25, where they represent the time given to the little horn to wear out the saints of the Most high and to change times and law. They correspond to the 1260 days of the concluding half-week of the Seventy Weeks.

This will bring to an end the persecution of the saints and the career of the Antichrist. But two extensions beyond this terminus are now mentioned, one of 30 days and another of 75 days. From the time the regular burnt offering is taken away and the abomination of desolation is set up (in the middle of the last week), there will be 1290 days, and blessed he who patiently waits until 1335 days have passed.

What might be expected at the end of these periods is not recorded, but I am attracted to the idea (Tregelles, Campbell) that thirty days will be spent in mourning while the rescued remnant of Israel learn the significance of the vicarious suffering of Christ and the enormity of their own wickedness in rejecting and crucifying their Messiah. Such a time of mourning is mentioned in Zechariah 12:10-14, and thirty days were spent in mourning after the death of Moses (Deuteronomy 34:8). It may be another 45 days before the tabernacle of David is set up as mentioned in Amos 9:11, but time alone will tell whether there is any truth in these guesses.

Go your way till the end

"But go your way till the end," Daniel is told. "And you shall rest and shall stand in your allotted place (lit. "your lot") at the end of the days." The lot is either the lot which is cast or the result of that casting, the place allotted, as in Judges 1:3 for example. We Christians will have our portion with "the lot of the saints in (the) light" (Colossians 1:12), "a lot among those who are sanctified by faith" in Christ (Acts 26:18). Daniel, for his part, will have his own allotted place in resurrection at the end of the days. His lot will be in that better, heavenly country where God has prepared for His people a city (Hebrews 11:16). There can be few who deserve their allotted place more than Daniel.

Conclusion

Daniel in prospect is not simply the way Daniel would have seen the future on the basis of the wisdom granted him; it is the way God intended it to be, the way it should have worked out if Israel had been submissive and believing. In Isaiah we find God's plan for Israel in the eighth century BC, in Jeremiah God's plan for that nation in the seventh century, and in Daniel God's plan for them, as seen in prospect, in the sixth century BC. Each plan is perfect in itself and could have been fulfilled in the manner revealed, but in point of fact each in turn was subsequently revised when Israel failed to respond in the way required and expected. Each successive plan was nevertheless a genuine offer which could have been fulfilled within the time-scale laid down if only Israel had repented and believed.

To Daniel was offered a prospect of future events which could (and should) have resulted in Messianic rest within 490 years of the going out of the word to restore and build Jerusalem. That word was initially expected in 536 BC at the close of the seventy years predicted for Babylon. But this word was delayed even in Daniel's lifetime, resulting in the head of gold (Babylon) being severed from the body, the first of several long delays in the fulfilment of Nebuchadnezzar's dream.

Eventually the decree to rebuild Jerusalem did go out in 445 BC, and the Seventy Weeks started out on its chequered career. After 69 weeks (483 luni-solar years) Messiah was cut off as Daniel had been shown, but the last week, the seventieth, did not follow on as expected. That was initially postponed for one generation only, because the Jews in crucifying their Messiah had acted in ignorance (Luke 23:34; Acts 3:17), and were consequently given another opportunity in which to repent and to rethink their position. By the end of Acts, however, the plea of ignorance could no longer be invoked (Romans 10:18-21; Acts 28:25-28). As a nation they had failed to repent and believe and must now face the consequences. For one thing, the last week of years was again postponed, this time for an indefinite period while God worked out His purpose among the Gentiles independently of Israel. For another, the Jews had once again to face the horror of the siege and destruction of Jerusalem and their own humiliating exile as slaves in distant and foreign lands.

What therefore might have been fulfilled within 490 years, now more than 2,500 years later still remains unfulfilled. But this is not God's doing; it is the result of man's folly and unbelief. It is not of God's doing, but is nevertheless part and parcel of God's overarching plan.

The image, as seen in prospect, conforms to the pattern of eight heads. The head itself, Babylon, lasted ideally for seventy years (Jeremiah 25:11-12; 29:10), and the rest of it for 490 years (Daniel 9:24). There is evidence that in the Greek world the ideal height of a man was regarded as eight heads. Lysippus, the fourth century Greek sculpture, is said to have "modified the Polycleitan rule that the head should equal one-seventh of the total height, adopting a ratio of 1:8." (A.W. Lawrence, *Classical Sculpture*, London 1929, p. 268). The futuristic dimensions of Nebuchadnezzar's dream are well suited to an image whose most important parts, the thighs legs and feet, stand for Greece and its successors.

The mutilated limbs of the image, as seen in retrospect, no longer exhibit any significant proportions. Not only is the head severed from the body, but the legs also are amputated at the thighs. The legs have never yet received a worthy fulfilment, and their fulfilment in the future may well be short and stubby compared with the elegant proportions as originally envisaged.

The main points

What therefore are the main points of this treatise? In the first place, predictive prophecy should never be regarded as pre-written history. The prophets were told how things ought to work out, assuming an attitude of submission and faith, not necessarily how it might otherwise turn out if these conditions were not fulfilled.

The second point springs from the first. It is that prophecy should always be interpreted prospectively from what is revealed, never retrospectively from recorded history. Only the prophet himself can tell us the meaning of the prophecy revealed to him. The third point is that prophecy in its very nature is conditional on the moral response of the people involved. If many prophecies have been repeatedly delayed and postponed it is entirely due to the human factor, the culpable unbelief of mankind in general, and especially of that stiff-necked people whom God chose for Himself.

But despite their hardness of heart God has not given up on His people Israel. One day soon He is going to take them up again, and then all those remarkable Old Testament prophecies will start to be fulfilled!

Appendix 1

Profile of the Prince to Come

There will be ten kings

Daniel 2:42 "And as the toes of the feet were partly iron and partly clay, so the kingdom shall be partly strong and partly brittle."

Daniel 7:24 "As for the ten horns, out of this kingdom ten kings shall arise..."

Revelation 13:1 "And I saw a beast rising out of the sea, with ten horns and seven heads, with ten diadems on its horns and blasphemous names on its heads."

Revelation 17:12 "And the ten horns that you saw are ten kings who have not yet received royal power, but they are to receive authority as kings for one hour, together with the beast."

Another horn, a little one

Daniel 7:8 "I considered the horns, and behold, there came up among them another horn, a little one, before which three of the first horns were plucked up by the roots."

Daniel 7:24 "and another (king) shall arise after them; he shall be different from the former ones, and shall put down three kings."

Daniel 8:9 "Out of one of them came a little horn, which grew exceedingly great towards the south, towards the east, and towards the glorious land."

Daniel 11:21-23 "In his place shall arise a contemptible person to whom royal majesty has not been given. He shall come in without warning and obtain the kingdom by flatteries..... he shall become strong with a small people."

Revelation 17:10-11 "They are also seven kings, five of whom are fallen.... As for the beast that was and is not, it is an eighth but it belongs to the seven, and it goes to destruction."

His authority will be recognised worldwide

Daniel 7:23 "it (the fourth kingdom) shall devour the whole earth, and trample it down, and break it to pieces."

Daniel 8:9-10 "Out of one of them came a little horn, which grew exceedingly great towards the south, towards the east, and towards the glorious land. It grew great, even to the host of heaven ..."

Revelation 13:7-8 "And authority was given it over every tribe and people and language and nation, and all who dwell on earth will worship it, everyone whose name has not been written before the foundation of the world in the book of life of the Lamb that was slain."

He will exalt himself and blaspheme against God

Daniel 7:8 "In this horn were eyes like the eyes of a man, and a mouth speaking great things."

Daniel 7:25 "He shall speak words against the Most High."

Daniel 8:23 "a king of bold countenance, one who understands riddles, shall arise."

Daniel 11:36 "He shall exalt himself and magnify himself above every god, and shall speak astonishing things against the God of gods."

Revelation 13:5-6 "And the beast was given a mouth uttering haughty and blasphemous words... It opened its mouth to utter blasphemies against God, blaspheming his name and his dwelling, that is, those who dwell in heaven."

He will exercise authority for a fixed period only

Daniel 7:25 "and they (the saints) shall be given into his hand for a time, times, and half a time."

Daniel 9:27 "for half of the week he shall put an end to sacrifice and offering."

Daniel 12:7 "it would be for a time, times, and half a time, and that when the shattering of the power of the holy people comes to an end all these things would be finished."

Revelation 12:14 "But the woman was given the two wings of the great eagle so that she might fly from the serpent into the wilderness, to the

place where she is to be nourished for a time, and times, and half a time". (*12:6* for 1,260 days.)
Revelation 13:5 "it was allowed to exercise authority for forty-two months."

He is allowed to destroy the saints (i.e. Israel is primarily in mind, but not exclusively)

Daniel 7:21 "this horn made war with the saints and prevailed over them."
Daniel 7:25 "he shall wear out the saints of the Most High."
Daniel 8:24 "he shall cause fearful destruction ... and destroy mighty men and the people who are the saints."
Daniel 9:26 "The coming prince will destroy (the) people, and their end shall be with a flood."
Daniel 11:33 "And the wise among the people shall make many understand, though for some days they shall stumble by sword and flame, by captivity and plunder."
Daniel 11:41 "He shall come into the glorious land, and tens of thousands shall fall."
Daniel 12:7 "when the shattering of the power of the holy people comes to an end all these things would be finished."
Revelation12:17 "Then the dragon became furious with the woman and went off to make war on the rest of her offspring, on those who keep the commandments of God and hold to the testimony of Jesus."
Revelation 13:7 "it was allowed to make war on the saints and to conquer them."

He will defile the Temple

Daniel 8:11 "And the regular burnt offering was taken away from Him, and the place of His sanctuary was overthrown"
Daniel 8:13-14 "For how long is the vision concerning the regular burnt offering, the transgression that makes desolate, and the giving over of the sanctuary and host to be trampled underfoot? And he said to me, 'For 2,300 evenings and mornings. Then the sanctuary shall be restored to its rightful state'."

Daniel 9:27 "and for half of the week he shall put an end to sacrifice and offering; and upon a wing (of the temple) shall be abominations which make desolate."

Daniel 11:31 "Forces from him shall appear and profane the temple (and) fortress, and shall take away the regular burnt offering. And they shall set up the abomination that makes desolate."

Daniel 12:11 "And from the time that the regular burnt offering is taken away and the abomination that makes desolate is set up, there shall be 1,290 days."

Revelation 11:1 "I was told, 'Rise and measure the temple of God and the altar and those who worship there, but do not measure the court outside the temple; leave that out, for it is given over to the nations, and they will trample the holy city for forty-two months.'"

Revelation 13:14-15 "it (the beast out of the earth) deceives those who dwell on the earth, telling them to make an image for the beast that was wounded by the sword and yet lived. And it was allowed to give breath to the image of the beast, so that the image of the beast might even speak and might cause those who would not worship the image of the beast to be slain."

He will come to an ignominious end

Daniel 7:26 "But the court shall sit in judgement, and his dominion shall be taken away, to be consumed and destroyed to the end."

Daniel 8:25 "And he shall even rise up against the Prince of princes, and he shall be broken - but by no human hand."

Daniel 9:27 "until the decreed end is poured out on the desolator."

Daniel 11:45 "And he shall pitch his palatial tent, between the sea and the glorious holy mountain. Yet he shall come to his end, with none to help him."

Revelation 17:14 "They (the beast and the ten kings) will make war on the Lamb, and the Lamb will conquer them, for he is Lord of lords and King of kings, and those with him are called and chosen and faithful.

Appendix 2

The Seventy Weeks

The critical view

In the view of the critical school the *terminus ad quem* of the Seventy Weeks, as of all the other visions in Daniel, is the death of Antiochus Epiphanes and the rededication of the Temple in 164 BC. The anointed one who is cut off is a reference to Onias III, the high priest put to death by Andronicus, the governor appointed by Antiochus, in 171 BC (2 Maccabees 4:23-35). The half-week indicates the three years of the profanation of the Temple, 168-165, concluding with the recovery and purification of the Temple by the Jews. The abomination of desolation is the heathen altar set up by Antiochus in the Temple, 1 Maccabees 1:54, where the words "abomination of desolation" are to be found.

The critics follow the Massoretic punctuation in separating the seven weeks from the sixty-two, and they differentiate between the two anointed ones. The anointed prince of verse 25 is either Cyrus or the high priest Jeshua, whereas the anointed one of verse 26 is Onias III. The first seven weeks correspond to the period of exile (586-538), and the following sixty-two weeks continue the story to the time of Antiochus. Montgomery is not at all embarrassed by the inexactness of the chronology, since "Jewish historiography was affected by a remarkable oblivion as to chronology and sequence of events."

He does however hold, in common with other scholars of his day, "that with the Seventy Weeks a definite, not intentionally indefinite, duration is meant, for how else could the divine 'word' satisfy Daniel's inquiry, v.2?" But more recent critics have taken the opposite view. In the view of Goldingay for example, "It is not chronology but chronography: a stylized scheme of history used to interpret historical data rather than arising from them, comparable to cosmology, arithmology, and genealogy as these appear in writings such as the OT." That being the case, the Seventy Weeks (7+62+1) is an artificial arrangement which does not convey any chronological information. This interpretation leaves no remainder for later times: it was all wrapped up and sealed in the second century BC.

The A-millennial view

The amillennial view takes various forms. Three will more than suffice: those of Keil, Young and Leupold. They are at least agreed on two things: that the numbers are purely symbolic, and that the *terminus a quo*, the starting point, is the edict of Cyrus as suggested by Isaiah 44:28.

Keil follows the Massoretic punctuation which separates the 7 weeks from the 62. The middle part of Daniel 9:25 he translates, "from the going forth of the command to restore and to build Jerusalem unto a Messiah, a prince, shall be seven weeks." These seven weeks, therefore, cover the period from the edict of Cyrus until the first coming of Christ.

The next part he translates, "And during threescore and two weeks it shall be restored and built, wide space and yet also limited, in the oppression of the times. And after the threescore and two weeks shall the Messiah be cut off, and it will not be to him (viz. that which he must have to be the Maschiah)." Hence the 62 weeks bridge the interval between the first and second comings of Christ. During this interval the city will be rebuilt, not however the earthly Jerusalem, but the city of God. It "refers to the preservation and extension of Jerusalem to the measure and compass determined by God in the Messianic time."

At the end of this period Messiah will be cut off. This cannot refer to the crucifixion since the Messianic age is by this time virtually over. It refers rather to "the annihilation of His place as Messiah." In consequence of this cutting off, destruction falls upon the city and sanctuary by the hands of the antichrist. So verse 27 refers to the action of the Antichrist at the end of the age.

Young and Leupold

Young understandably disagrees with Keil on a number of points. For a start he is not happy with the Massoretic punctuation. "This violent separation of the two periods is out of harmony with the context", he says. He correctly understands the text as stating that "between the *terminus a quo* and the appearance of an anointed one, a prince, is a period of 69 sevens which is divided into periods of unequal length, 7 sevens and 62 sevens." The first seven were fulfilled between the issuance of the word and the completion of the city and temple, roughly to the end of the period of Ezra and Nehemiah. And the 62 sevens follow on from this.

As for the cutting off of the anointed one, "The old evangelical interpretation is that which alone satisfies the requirements of the case. The 'anointed one' is Jesus Christ, who is cut off by His death upon the Cross of Calvary." He also disagrees with Keil over the prince who is to come. "It seems most likely that the 'people' are the Romans, and the prince who is to come is Titus Vespasianus."

Verse 27 reverts to the work of Christ in Young's opinion. Our Lord fulfilled the terms of the Covenant of Grace, on the basis of which life and salvation are freely offered to sinners. It was moreover Messiah who by His death on the cross caused sacrifice and oblation to cease. Conversely, the one making desolate is another reference to Titus who destroyed the Temple after the end of the seventieth week, "consequent upon the action of the Messiah in causing the sacrifice and oblation to cease."

"Thus, since the Messiah has caused sacrifice and oblation to cease, there comes a desolator over the temple, and devastation continues until a full, determined end pours forth upon the desolation." On this interpretation the prophecy is exhausted in AD 70. Nothing it says reaches beyond that point.

Leupold is in agreement with Keil on all essential points, including the anomaly of Christ being cut off sometime in the future. Not least of the merits of this interpretation, in his view, is that it refuses to make mathematical computations. He offers no explanation why 7 heptads should be allocated to the period between the edict of Cyrus and the coming of Christ, and then 62 heptads for the duration of the Church age. If the numbers carry no significance, why 62? Why use numbers at all if they do not convey any meaning? They are in any case disproportionate. If 7 heptads corresponds to 500 years, 62 heptads would suggest something in the region of 4,500 years. Will the Church age really go on that long?

The amillennial school are quick to affirm their commitment to the inspiration of the Bible, but strangely slow to believe what it says. They are far too prone to spirit away the plain meaning of the text - they call it 'spiritualizing' - on the pretext that the Bible cannot be taken at its face value. Without more ado I shall now turn to the type of interpretation which I myself find acceptable.

Sir Robert Anderson

A major breakthrough was made in the understanding of the Seventy Weeks by Sir Robert Anderson in *The Coming Prince* (5th edition, 1895). Anderson took as the starting-point the decree of Artaxerxes' twentieth year, 445 BC. This date we have already found to be the most satisfactory. Assuming the decree was issued on the first day of the month Nisan, though the text does not actually say so (Nehemiah 2:1), Anderson calculated that from that day to Palm Sunday AD 32, when Jesus was acclaimed Messiah and Prince, was precisely 173,880 days, that is 483 years (69 weeks of years), assuming the years were luni-solar years of 360 days each.

Anderson rightly says that Ist Nisan in AD 32 should have been 1st April, and consequently 15 Nisan should have fallen on 15 April. With this Parker and Dubberstein, whose tables are generally considered authoritative, are in complete agreement. These facts, however, did not suit Anderson's calculation, so he assumed a residue of four days left over after the end of an assumed leap month. In this way he found reason to advance 1st Nisan in this year to Friday 28 March. On the basis of this revised dating his calculation would seem to be correct.

But why should the years be ones of 360 days, a year-length never used in Israel or anywhere else? The reason is that the seventieth week, which was subsequently cut off from the previous sixty-nine, is divided in the book of Revelation into two half-weeks of 1260 days or 42 months, that is three and a half years of 360 days or 42 months of 30 days. The Beast of Revelation 13:5 is quite clearly the same person as the little horn of Daniel 7:8 and 8:9, the wilful king of Daniel 11:36, and the coming prince of Daniel 9:27. The same things are said of each of them: that they speak great things and blasphemies, that they make war on the saints and overcome them, that they defile the Temple courts, etc. The Beast is allowed to exercise authority for 42 months (Revelation 13:5), the coming prince for half the last week of years (Daniel 9:27), and the little horn for a time, times and half a time (Daniel 7:25). These are all equivalent to 1260 days as Revelation makes clear (11:2-3; 12:6,14).

Anderson says, "The only data which would warrant our deciding unreservedly that the prophetic year consists of 360 days would be to find some portion of the era subdivided into the days of which it is composed. No other proof can be wholly satisfactory, but if this is forthcoming, it must be absolute and conclusive. And this is precisely what the book of Revelation gives us" (p.72).

I cannot find fault with this reasoning. If it is proved that the last week of years is reckoned in a certain way, it must follow that the preceding sixty-nine weeks are reckoned in the same way. According to Lucas, "It is very unlikely that anyone would have used a 360-day year in chronological calculations." But this is not a chronological calculation in the usual sense; it is a prophetic forecast intentionally cryptic, similar to the enigmatic "time, times and dividing of times." The meaning was not supposed to be immediately obvious, and it is only in the light of subsequent revelation that the precise meaning becomes clear.

Points of disagreement

Anderson's interpretation is open to the following criticisms.

(1) His invention of an "ecclesiastical moon" four days in advance of the true moon (p.103) is a blunder of the first order. He tries to hide up the weakness of his position by this fictitious invention, which only serves to obscure the fact that AD 32 is the one year which astronomy actually excludes completely.

(2) Anderson also erred in thinking the Crucifixion took place on 15 Nisan whereas it was really 14 Nisan, the day before the Jewish Passover. If 14 Nisan is to fall on a Friday, the first of the month has to be a Saturday. But in AD 32 that was not the case, and consequently 14 Nisan was not a Friday. J.K. Fotheringham has this to say, "In 32 Nisan 14 should have fallen on Sunday April 13, or Monday April14. It is absolutely impossible to shift this to a Thursday or Friday" (1934: 160).

(3) There is wide acceptance that the true year of the Crucifixion was AD 33, but this year is one too late so far as Anderson's calculations are concerned. See for example Jack Finegan's *Handbook of Biblical Chronology*, revised edition 1998.

The year of the Crucifixion most probably AD 33

But could it be that the authorities have picked on the wrong month? In any given year there is no absolute certainty which month was reckoned as the first month in Judea. Could it be that in 32 Nisan was really the month preceding the one assumed by Fotheringham and others? For the month preceding, Parker and Dubberstein give 2 March, a Sunday, as the first of the month. In that month the new moon did not rise in Jerusalem until about 9:30 pm on 29 February, and by that time 1st March would have already begun in Judea. The first of the new month might have been Sunday 2 March or Monday 3 March, but it cannot have been Saturday 1st March. Barring some very exceptional circumstance, 32 is the one year which astronomy appears to exclude as a feasible year of the Crucifixion.

When however we turn our attention to AD 33 there is no problem at all. In that year 1st Nisan could well have been Saturday 21 March, and 14 Nisan Friday 3 April. This month is given as Second Adar AD 32, a leap month, by Parker and Dubberstein, but there is absolutely no reason why it should not have been counted as Nisan 33 by the Jews. It is therefore with good reason that many modern scholars have accepted 33 as the most probable year of the Crucifixion.

What is the answer?

One way of salvaging Anderson's calculation is to assume that Artaxerxes' twentieth year, as reckoned by the Jews, was really 444 BC, rather than 445. This assumption is made by Harold Hoehner among others in *Chronological Aspects of the Life of Christ* (1977). Nisan 444 to AD 33 would produce approximately the same result as 445 to AD 32. But is this assumption justified? The answer has to be No! It is well established that the Jews employed antedating, not postdating, when reckoning the reigns of kings both native and foreign. These were reckoned from Tishri (the seventh month) preceding the true date of accession, not the Tishri following. Thus Nebuchadnezzar's first year was reckoned from Nisan 604 in Babylon, but from Tishri 605 in Israel. Likewise Artaxerxes' first year was reckoned from Nisan 464 in Persia, but from Tishri 465 in Israel. Artaxerxes' twentieth year had already begun in Kislev (the ninth month) 446 as reckoned in Nehemiah (Nehemiah 1:1), and was still in progress in Nisan 445 (2:1).

As I understand it, the 69 weeks of Daniel's prophecy did in fact run out in Nisan AD 32. The Crucifixion should have taken place in that year, but in response to Christ's petition the Jews were given one more year in which to show the fruits of repentance. Hence the Crucifixion was postponed by one year, one year beyond the limit set by Daniel. Our Lord's appeal is expressed in the Parable of the Barren Fig-tree in Luke 13:6-9:

> And he told this parable: "A man had a fig tree planted in his vineyard, and he came seeking fruit on it and found none. And he said to the vine dresser, 'Look, for three years now I have come seeking fruit on this fig tree, and I find none. Cut it down. Why should it use up the ground? And he answered him, 'Sir, let it alone this year also, until I dig round it and put on manure. Then if it should bear fruit next year, well and good; but if not, you can cut it down.'"

The owner asked for one more year, and this request was granted. This would suggest that our Lord's ministry was extended by one year, from three years to four, and consequently it was not until AD 33 that He died.

It was during this year that He made His long roundabout journey to Jerusalem which takes up nearly half of Luke's Gospel, 9:51-19:27.It should always be remembered that prophecy is conditional in character, and it is especially in the time element that this conditionality is witnessed. The prophecy of the Seventy Weeks should have begun in 536 with the decree of Cyrus, but the starting point was postponed. It was ninety-one years later that it eventually began. Again, it should have ended in AD 39, seven years after the cutting off of Messiah at the end of the sixty-ninth week. But the last week of years, unbeknown to Daniel, was subsequently removed from its rightful place and still to this day lies sometime in the future. It should not surprise us therefore if the cutting off of Messiah was itself postponed by one year. The event itself was never in doubt, even the year seemed to be fixed. But history is full of surprises: this year too was delayed by twelve months as we now know in retrospect.

What is the cause of all these delays? It is of course the human factor, man's failure to repent, his indifference, his failure to respond in the manner expected, and above all his rejection of the promised Messiah. There was no way that God could fulfil His gracious promises when provoked in this way.

The importance of this prophecy

The importance of these Seventy Weeks for the understanding of hermeneutic principles in general, and Daniel in particular, cannot be emphasized too much. These weeks should have begun in 536 through the instrumentality of Cyrus. They would then have ended 490 luni-solar years later - in 53 BC! This is what Daniel would have expected in the first year of Darius (538), assuming he understood the import of the message and the nature of the years.

Daniel may not have been surprised when Cyrus' decree made no mention of the city. Knowing the mentality of his countrymen he may well have suspected that the starting-point would be postponed. When it did eventually begin in the twentieth year of Artaxerxes Daniel himself had been dead for nearly ninety years. Again, viewed in prospect, the period should have ended in AD 39, seven years after the cutting off of

Messiah. No-one could have foreseen that the last week of years would be displaced from the sixty-ninth. The rejection and violent death of Messiah were foreseen by the prophets Daniel and Isaiah. What they did not foresee was the universality of His rejection by the Jews. It was this which caused a rupture in their relationship with God and the postponement of their national hopes.

Bibliography of Books and Commentaries

The following books and commentaries have been referred to or quoted in the text.

Critical

Robert A. Anderson, *Signs and Wonders: A Commentary on the Book of Daniel*, Eerdmans 1984.

Robert H. Charles, *A Critical and Exegetical Commentary on the Book of Daniel*, Oxford 1929.

S.R. Driver, *The Book of Daniel*, Cambridge Bible for Schools and Colleges, Cambridge 1900.

F.W. Farrar, *The Book of Daniel*, The Expositor's Bible, Eerdmans 1943.

John E. Goldingay, *Word Biblical Commentary 30: Daniel*, Dallas 1989.

Ernest C. Lucas, *Apollos Old Testament Commentary 20: Daniel*, Illinois 2002.

James A. Montgomery, *A Critical and Exegetical Commentary on the Book of* Daniel (ICC), T.& T. Clark Edinburgh 1927.

H. H. Rowley, *Darius the Mede and the Four World Empires in the Book of Daniel*, Cardiff 1935.

A- (and Post-) millennial

C. F. Keil, *Biblical Commentary on the Book of Daniel*, Eerdmans reprint, no date.

H. C. Leupold, *Exposition of Daniel*, Baker Book House, reprinted 1969.

Ronald S. Wallace, *The Message of Daniel: The Lord is King*, Inter-Varsity Press 1979.

Edward J. Young, *The Prophecy of Daniel: A Commentary*, Eerdmans 1949.

Pre-millennial

(Sir) Robert Anderson, *The Coming Prince*, 5th edition, London 1895.

William Campbell, Th*e Prophecies of Daniel*, Auckland, N.Z. 1973.

William Kelly, *Notes on the Book of Daniel*, London 1897.

A. E. Knoch, *Concordant Studies in the Book of Daniel*, California 1968.

G. H. Lang, *The Histories and Prophecies of Daniel*, Paternoster 1950.

C. G. Ozanne, *The Fourth Gentile Kingdom (in Daniel and Revelation)*, Worthing 1982.

G. H. Pember, *The Great Prophecies of the Centuries concerning Israel and the Gentiles*, London 1895.

S. P. Tregelles, *Remarks on the Prophetic Visions in the Book of Daniel*, 7th edition, Sovereign Grace Advent Testimony 1965 (First published in 1852).

John F, Walvoord, *Daniel: The Key to Prophetic Revelation*, Moody 1971.

Leon Wood, *A Commentary on Daniel*, Zondervan 1973.

Uncommitted

Daniel Berrigan, *Daniel: Under the Siege of the Divine*, Plough Publishing House, PA 1998.

Ron Cantrell, *The Final Kingdom Where all Kingdoms bow to the Ancient of Days*, Jerusalem 2000.

Other Works

A. B. Davidson, *Old Testament Prophecy*, T.&T. Clark, Edinburgh 1905.

J.K. Fotheringham, "The Evidence of Astronomy and Technical Chronology for the Date of the Crucifixion", *Journal of Theological Studies* 35 (1934), 142-162.

R.A. Parker and W.H. Dubberstein, *Babylonian Chronology 626 B.C. - A.D. 75*, Second edition, Providence 1956.

D. J. Wiseman, *Nebuchadrezzar and Babylon*, Schweich Lectures for 1983, Oxford 1985.

About the Author

Charles Ozanne was born in Crowborough, Sussex, in 1936. He read Theology at Oxford before undertaking research in the book of Revelation for his PhD at the University of Manchester under F. F. Bruce. Some of his recent publications for the Open Bible Trust have been a critique of Replacement Theology entitled *God's Plan for Israel: Replacement or Restoration?* And a work looking at *The Sabbath and Circumcision*.

His latest major work is *Understanding the New Testament*. A well-written and well-presented commentary on the whole of the New Testament, showing that each of the 27 documents, although distinctive, fit into an overall pattern. For further details of this latest book, and others, please visit:

www.obt.org.uk

Charles Ozanne us a regular contributor to Search magazine

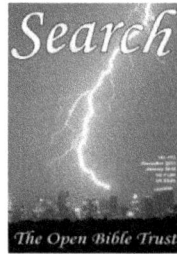

For a free sample of the Open Bible Trust's magazine Search, Please email admin@obt.org.uk or visit

www.obt.org.uk/search

Also by Charles Ozanne

Charles Ozanne has written a number of books on the Minor Prophets which are available as eBooks. These include:

Hosea: Prophet to Israel – The Northern Kingdom
Nahum's Vision Concerning Nineveh
Malachi: The Lord's Messenger
Joel and the Day of the Lord
The Book of Immanuel (Isaiah 7-12)
Amos: The Lion has roared

Further details of these can be seen on www.obt.org.uk
They can be ordered from that website.

They are available as eBooks from Amazon and Apple and also as
KDP paperbacks from Amazon

·

More on Prophecy

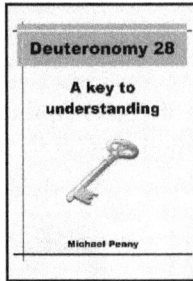

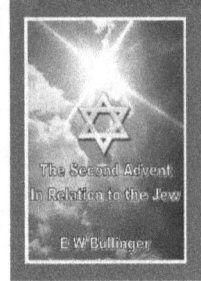

Apocalypse: Introduction to Revelation
Brian Sherring

Deuteronomy 28: A key to understanding
Michael Penny

Christ's Prophetic Teaching
E W Bullinger

The Second Advent in Relation to the Jew
E W Bullinger

**Revelation: The Most Tremendous Book
in the world
William Campbell
(2 volumes)**

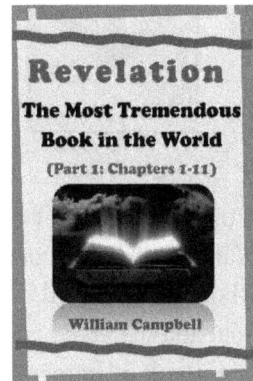

Further details of these can be seen on www.obt.org.uk
They can be ordered from that website.

They are available as eBooks from Amazon and Apple and also as
KDP paperbacks from Amazon